Ian Phillips

London.

82/83

**Foreign Exchange
and the
Corporate Treasurer**

# Foreign Exchange and the Corporate Treasurer

JOHN HEYWOOD

THIRD EDITION, REVISED AND EXTENDED

**Adam & Charles Black**

LONDON

Third edition 1981
First published 1978
A & C Black (Publishers) Ltd
35 Bedford Row, London WC1R 4JH
ISBN 0–7136–2185–0

Heywood, John
    Foreign exchange and the corporate treasurer.
    3rd ed. rev. and extended
    1. Foreign exchange
    I. Title
    332.4'5'02465      HG3826

    ISBN 0-7136-2185-0

Printed in Great Britain by
Biddles Ltd, Guildford, Surrey

# Contents

# Preface

For some years now I have been responsible for the foreign exchange operations of Hambros Bank Ltd in London. In my daily work I have come across a great variety of customers' foreign exchange problems, from a customer using the foreign exchange market for the first time to the sophisticated policy decisions of the major multinationals. It has been this continuous exposure to customers' problems that gradually convinced me that there was a place for a book of this kind. It is intended to provide an introduction and reference source in the subject for all those accountants, export salesmen, buyers, and executives who now find that decisions about foreign exchange have become a necessary part of their job, as well as being a general text on the subject for colleges and business schools.

So firstly, I am indebted to Hambros Bank Ltd and its customers for the opportunity to acquire experience in this field by that most direct of methods, 'learning by doing'. Further, it must be said that although I was able to recognise the customer's need for a book on this subject, it took me very much longer to come to realise that if I wanted such a book to exist then I was going to have to write one myself. When, rather apprehensively, I decided to do this, assistance was immediately at hand from all sides.

I would like to acknowledge the help and encouragement received both from Hambros Bank Ltd and from many friends in the foreign exchange and money markets in London, the USA, Scandinavia and the Continent, both in assisting to formulate ideas and in confirming particular points of detail.

My specific thanks go to Kenneth Dibben, Graham Steward and Bob Thomas who gave their time to read and comment on my text and to Margaret Wood who typed it.

Finally, my thanks go to my wife, Diane, who patiently accepted the large demands on my time that writing any book necessarily entails.

# Preface to Third Edition

It is now four years since I sat down to write the first edition of this book. In that time the foreign exchange markets have continued to expand and develop, and Corporate Treasurers have come to play an increasingly important and well recognised role in companies. New treasury techniques have been developed and older ones refined.

This third edition thus provides an opportunity to take account of the rapid and diverse changes that have taken place in this field. The initial introductory sections of the book and the various appendices have been updated throughout. But the basic change from the earlier editions concerns the second half of the book which is almost entirely rewritten. New, much expanded sections outline recent developments in Currency Invoicing, Translation Exposure and methods of Treasury Organisation.

A new chapter describes Currency Exchange Agreements, a subject that scarcely existed when the first edition was being written. Similarly, another four years of experience of changing market developments have led to a better appreciation of the merits of the various different currency forecasting techniques. This section too has been rewritten based on the new work in this field by international economists and bankers.

I again acknowledge the helpful advice and suggestions from many friends – foreign exchange dealers and managers, Corporate Treasurers and finance directors in the United Kingdom, the USA, Scandinavia and the Continent – whose contribution to the debate in this subject area continues to help me to clarify ideas and to refine them in the light of experience; in short, to learn.

**For Richard and Louise**

# 1 Why Foreign Exchange matters more than it used to

Some form of foreign exchange market is necessary for the development of any international trade beyond the stage of barter. For this reason such markets have been in existence for several thousand years. The markets have not developed in a steady manner and like most industries have had many setbacks on the way. Indeed the only memorable reference to foreign exchange dealing activities in the Bible describes the money changers being thrown out of the temple. Although it may be felt that this story would cast a rather unfortunate negative image over the profession, it continued to develop in line with the steady increase in international trade over the centuries, and has continued to do so right up to the present day. It may be wondered why a market which has been in existence in gradually developing form for thousands of years should suddenly, in the space of only ten years or so, assume such a radically greater importance. To show why this is so, it is necessary briefly to trace the history of international monetary affairs since the Bretton Woods agreement of 1944.

At that time the US dollar was convertible into gold at the fixed rate of \$35 per ounce. This rate had been fixed by the US Government in 1934. At Bretton-Woods sterling was fixed relative to the US dollar at US \$4·03 = £1 and therefore also had a known 'gold parity'. In turn nearly all the principal world currencies were fixed in value either to the dollar or to sterling or both, and thus indirectly to gold. In 1949 the British Government devalued the pound to \$2·80 and those currencies linked to sterling automatically followed suit. A further devaluation to \$2·40 occurred in November 1967. These arrangements remained in force more or less intact until 1971 and the entire period was one of reasonable stability in foreign exchange matters. But from then on this tidy structure gradually began to fall apart. To list the main events only:

- In mid 1971 the United States suspended the convertibility of US dollars into gold.
- The Deutsche Mark (DMark) was 'floated' and no longer kept a fixed rate against the US dollar.
- In December 1971 the Smithsonian Agreement provided a general realignment of currency values. Sterling was fixed at $2·6057, the DMark was refixed against the US dollar. But currencies were now permitted a fluctuation of $2\frac{1}{4}\%$ either side of the new parities compared with 1% hitherto.
- In April 1972 several European currencies began the 'Snake' Agreement whereby they agreed that the permitted fluctuation between members would also be confined to $\pm2\frac{1}{4}\%$.
- In June 1972 sterling left the snake to float independently and started to fall in value. Countries with currencies linked to sterling had to decide whether to follow sterling down or float independently. Some chose one course, some the other.
- In February 1973 the dollar was devalued. Again some countries followed and some did not. Several total closures of the markets followed as individual central banks decided on new policies for the value of their own currency. The lira was floated independently.
- In March 1973 the various European currencies which had fixed parities relative to each other and to the dollar decided to break the link with the dollar maintaining only the relationship amongst themselves. Even this island of stability was broken in June when the DMark revalued again.

Finally, in October 1973 'the OPEC crisis' arose when the members of the OPEC countries quadrupled the price of oil to the industrial countries. This created all manner of major repercussions throughout the financial world. In this situation where the formal links that had held the currencies together, and which had contributed so much to the earlier stability, were already being dismantled, this new crisis proved very hard for the market to absorb. From then on the world has experienced currency crises of increasing frequency and scale. Exchange rates have moved further, faster and more frequently than had been known within the business lifetime of most people now working in industry.

There may well be those who say that of course 'everyone knows' that the foreign exchanges are more unstable than they used to be, but perhaps it is worth stopping to take a look at the numbers. These are in fact quite alarming when seen in the cold light of day. For example, the table below shows the maximum movement in exchange rate of the Norwegian krone against sterling experienced during a quarter, a month, and a day for 1974, 1975 and 1976.

**Maximum Movement in Exchange Rate**
**Norwegian Krone against Sterling, %**

|                              | 1974 | 1975 | 1976   | 1977 | 1978 | 1979 |
|------------------------------|------|------|--------|------|------|------|
| Within the year              | 6·5  | 20·0 | 36·0*  | 15·3 | 7·8  | 15·1 |
| Worst 3 months               | 3·1  | 9·7  | 20·5   | 10·4 | 6·9  | 11·4 |
| Worst month                  | 2·8  | 7·7  | 7·6    | 4·8  | 6·6  | 6·5  |
| Worst day                    | 1·5  | 2·4  | 2·8    | 3·4  | 5·6  | 2·3  |
| Exchange rate at mid year    | 13·0 | 11·4 | 9·7    | 9·1  | 10·0 | 11·1 |

* In case this figure of 36% seems hard to believe, the historical rates are easy to check. The rate was at its maximum of 11·30 on 9 January, and the low of 8·28 was recorded on 28 October.

It will be seen that the maximum movement recorded in a day rose from 1·5% to nearly 3% and the maximum movement recorded in three months rose from 3·1% in 1974 to over 20% in 1976. It will be noticed from the table that the figures shown are those for the Norwegian krone against sterling. The reader may well feel that these two currencies were chosen because these were the worst in order to make the point. Unfortunately, they were by no means the worst, DMarks against sterling for instance would have shown far greater movements than those in the table. The point the figures are intended to illustrate is that these movements are very large, that they continue to increase in size, speed, and frequency, and that for several years each succeeding year has been worse than the previous ones in terms of most measures of exchange market stability.

This increase in both the size and speed of changes has been enough to change the nature of the problem faced by companies. If the problems change so must the most appropriate solutions, and so must the priority given to efforts to solve the problems. One is still constantly amazed at the discrepancy between the amount of effort a company is prepared to devote to reducing the production cost of its products by say one half of 1% – often involving large teams of production engineers, work study analysts, inventory controllers, and so on, when ten times as much margin can so easily be thrown away by a casual approach to handling currency exposures. Perhaps as time goes by the effort devoted to these two areas of business decisions will become more commensurate with the likely return from each.

The economic environment now facing the financial executive contains at least two major new uncertainties – inflation and exchange rate instability. To neglect either in today's financial planning is to neglect present day economic realities. This is the real and compelling reason for taking an increased interest in the mechanics of the foreign exchange market.

# 2 How Foreign Exchange Deals arise

Business is gradually becoming more and more international. It has become a worldwide trend for companies to expand and to spread their risk amongst many countries and markets. More and more of them cross frontiers for customers, sources of supply and investment. But all cross-frontier trade inevitably gives rise to foreign exchange exposure for somebody.

This basic fact may be simply illustrated thus. Consider the rather simple example of a man who wishes to purchase machinery from West Germany. We will assume that the purchaser is in the UK and has the choice of the currency in which he should buy and pay for the machines. Basically he has three choices here, he may either agree to buy in terms of sterling or DMarks or some other currency.

It may seem that if he purchases in sterling then there is no foreign exchange problem arising, but the foreign exchange problem then arises for the seller of the machine. He will be in receipt of sterling and will wish to sell it for DMarks on his local market. If on the other hand the machine is invoiced in DMarks, then the buyer will first have to buy the DMarks with which to buy the machine. Either way a foreign exchange transaction is involved for somebody. If the goods are invoiced in a third currency, for instance US dollars, then first of all the English buyer must buy the US dollars and arrange payment in US dollars to the German supplier. In turn the German supplier must then sell the dollars and convert into DMarks to pay his local expenses in producing the machine. In this event we have two foreign exchange deals to do, in the previous cases only one.

As has been said, it is axiomatic that any movement of goods or services across a frontier will give rise to a foreign exchange transaction for somebody. Of course, not all foreign exchange transactions arise out of the sale of goods; the sale of services – for instance in tourism, or banking, or insurance – will also involve payments between one country and another for these services giving similar foreign exchange transactions through the market place. A further type of transaction is where a company in one country purchases a foreign capital asset, perhaps a business or property, and so requires to buy the funds for that capital purchase across the frontier.

These examples are all fairly clear and might be supposed to form the bulk of the transactions going through foreign exchange markets at any given time. But much other business is also going through the market every day. For instance, supposing a company in Denmark borrows Swiss francs to be used in financing its domestic business. Having confirmed the date and amount the company will sell the Swiss francs to buy Danish kroner for use in the business. Every time an interest payment or a repayment on the loan is due, the company will buy the necessary Swiss francs on the market. Such financial transactions are a major feature of the market today.

All these transactions provide the initial input to the market, since they are usually made between a corporate customer and his bank. The bank of course is trading all day to 'lay off' these initial deals and to keep its books in balance. So a large number of secondary deals is released into the market as banks seek to trade off the business put to them by customers. Some banks specialise in this secondary business, providing a service to the customer-based banks and adding to the depth of the market. Their provision of a smoothly acting and efficient secondary market enables the primary market to operate more effectively too.

The net result of all this activity on a given day may be to cause a particular currency to be in temporary but strong demand. Such price fluctuations may cause two other types of participant to come into the market – market speculators may feel that the price is an anomaly which provides a possible profit opportunity, or the central bank of the currency concerned may decide to intervene in the market to stabilise the rate.

Because of the scale of financial, secondary, speculative and intervention transactions, the number of foreign exchange transactions between companies and banks for payment for goods as a proportion of all foreign exchange transactions done by banks is normally small. Despite this, most deals done by banks are in fact directly or indirectly in support of the basic international trade functions of the market, even in the case of those banks who concentrate almost entirely on the secondary or 'interbank' sector of the market.

# 3 Basic Building Blocks

There tends to be a lot of mystique – and jargon! – surrounding the subject of foreign exchange and as a result there is a tendency for the layman to believe that it must be much more complex than is actually the case. However, there is one simple truth that usually helps the layman penetrate the fog with a little more confidence. It is that, despite the many centuries of evolution, only four types of deal have so far come into existence:

1 BORROW
2 LEND
3 BUY
4 SELL

There are no others.

If the basic mechanics of these four types of deal can be followed through in detail then many of the problems of the subject are stripped away. All the other more sophisticated types of transaction we shall go on to discuss in this book are merely combinations of the above four basic transactions. So it is vital to understand with some precision how each of these four basic building blocks work. Of course, having done that we will still have to learn how to use them. Like notes of music there are many ways in which these basic building blocks can be arranged in combination to good or ill effect. We all know that the schoolboy sitting at a piano has, in theory, the same notes at his disposal as Chopin. The reason he may not get the same results is concerned with sequence, timing, and the use of combinations.

In order to understand the basic mechanics, we must first define our terms.

**Money Means Bank Deposits**

Firstly, when we talk of 'currency' or 'money' we do not mean banknotes, travellers cheques, or coin. These cash items are not handled in the foreign exchange market but through the parallel market of the Bureaux de Change. 'Currency' or 'money' means money on a bank account. In a national sense most of a country's stock of money is made up of money on bank accounts and the cash items are relatively small. (From the point of view of the banking system, cash items are merely money in transit from one bank account to another. This is readily apparent if one considers what will happen to the cash in one's own pocket. First it is spent, say in a shop, and then the shopkeeper pays in the cash to his bank where it is converted into a balance on his bank account.)

Secondly, all bank deposits are ultimately on deposit in the home country of the currency. That is, all dollar deposits on deposit with a bank are in the USA, all French francs with a bank in France and so on. It is this statement that is one of the major difficulties for those unfamiliar with international banking payments. People are aware that they see the rates of interest which London banks will pay for US dollar deposits quoted in the financial press, and this knowledge seems at first sight to be irreconcilable with the above statement. What they often do not realise is that all dollar deposits placed with European banks have to be effected by paying the dollar funds into the European bank's *own* bank account with its United States bankers. Thus all movements of funds over dollar accounts anywhere in the world are paralleled by exactly equivalent movements over the non-US banks' own dollar bank accounts in the USA.

### Mechanics of a Dollar Deposit with a Bank outside the USA

Because a clear understanding of these principles is so important to what will follow later on, it is worth while to trace in some detail what actually happens when an industrial company puts US $1 million on deposit with, say, a London bank. Let us suppose the company is Deutsche Industrie AG, Frankfurt, and it is to receive the money in payment for export of machine tools to the USA. Deutsche Industrie's cash flow picture is such that the money is not immediately required and so it is decided to place it on a one month fixed deposit. The dollars will be paid to Deutsche Industrie AG in a few days' time, and their customer confirms that, as per contract, payment will be made to Deutsche Industrie's New York bank account at ABC Bank, New York.

Deutsche Industrie then asks two or three international banks with whom they regularly deal to quote interest rates for their one month dollar deposit. The company might for instance call one bank in Luxembourg, one in Zurich and one in London. We will suppose that on this occasion they decide to deal with London Bank Ltd at an agreed interest rate. When the rate is agreed the company will ask the bank, 'Where do you want your dollars?' The bank may then reply, 'Please pay our dollars to First National Bank of Anywhere, New York, for account of London Bank Ltd for account of Deutsche Industrie AG'. The first may then finish off with, 'OK, the dollars come from ABC Bank, New York, please repay principal and interest there on maturity. We will confirm deal and instructions by telex.'

The monetary effect of all this is that the dollar balance on Deutsche Industrie AG's account at ABC Bank in New York has moved to London Bank Ltd's account at First National Bank of Anywhere in New York. The dollars always exist as a balance on a bank account at a US bank.

The contractual effect of course looks different. Deutsche Industrie AG has made a contract with London Bank Ltd to provide that bank with the use of US $1 million in New York for one month, at a certain rate of interest and that contract is recorded in the books of London Bank.

But the dollars are not in London and it is in fact impossible for them to be in London. For most practical purposes in a foreign exchange market context, it may be assumed that all US dollars are balances at banks in New York City.

London Bank Ltd now has to decide what to do with this US $1 million deposited by its German customer. The simplest alternative is to lend it to someone, let us say a French bank – Banque Française de Dépôts is interested at the time. This bank may have a New York branch and will ask for 'his' dollars to be paid there. London Bank Ltd has now done one dollar deposit and one dollar loan and its balance at its account at First National Bank of Anywhere, New York, will be at the same level as at the beginning. He has made two contracts and has secured a margin between the deposit and loan rate for the one month period. No funds have moved in Frankfurt, Paris or London, as the only currency involved was the dollar which, as we have said, may be considered as being in New York at all times.

**Mechanics of a Foreign Exchange Deal**

Having now considered what happens to transact a loan and a deposit, we can go on to consider a foreign exchange transaction. A foreign exchange deal is a contract to exchange a bank balance in one currency for a bank balance in another currency at an agreed price for settlement on an agreed date.

Let us take the example of a customer wishing to buy French francs and to sell US dollars, and for simplicity we will assume that the rate of exchange is FF4·00 = $1, the customer is buying FF6 million for settlement on 18 May and has a dollar account at ABC Bank in New York.

The deal will usually be done by telephone. After some initial discussion London Bank Ltd's dealer's agreement to deal may be expressed thus:

> 'OK then, we sell you French francs six million and buy the dollars for value 18 May at a rate of 4·00 00. Please pay our dollars to our account at First National Bank of Anywhere, New York. Where do you want your French francs?'

The customer replies:

> 'Please pay our French francs to Banque Française de Dépôts, Paris, for account of our supplier Compagnie Lebrun et Frères SA quoting reference "shipment of olive oil invoice N/11642/AP". We pay the dollars from ABC Bank, New York. We will confirm the deal and the payment instructions by telex within the next hour.'

> 'Fine, that's noted – thanks for the deal.'

The total time involved will usually be less than one minute. The effect is that a contract has been made to exchange a dollar bank balance for a French franc bank balance. Also, of course, funds belonging to the customer will now be provided to his supplier in discharge of his debt for the goods supplied.

But there are still a few things that have to be done to give effect to the contract made:

> *a*: London Bank will telex its own correspondent bank in France and instruct them to pay FF6 million from their account to their customer's supplier's bank as agreed.

    *b*: The customer will telex ABC Bank instructing them to pay $1·5 million to First National Bank of Anywhere for account of London Bank Ltd.

    *c*: The customer will telex confirm the date, rate and amount of the deal done together with the relative payment instructions. This is in all respects merely a confirmation, the contract was the verbal agreement on the telephone.

Meanwhile the bank has probably dealt in the interbank market to buy FF6 million against dollars or 'laid off' the deal in the market, so as to square their position again.

The many variations, refinements, conventions, risks, safeguards and controls that in practice underlie these basic deals provide the main subject matter of the rest of this book.


**Spot Date**

The normal foreign exchange deal done in the market is for 'value spot'. This means that the contract will be settled on the 'spot' date which is normally set two days ahead of the day on which the deal is done. This two day period allows time for the various payment instructions to be exchanged and effected and for any exchange control formalities to be cleared.

However, the determination of 'spot' date can be complicated by holidays. It is not possible to effect settlement of a foreign exchange deal on a day which is a bank holiday in the country of either currency concerned. Equally it is not usual to settle foreign exchange transactions on days which are New York holidays, even where the dollar is not involved. This is because most of the market conventionally deals each currency against the US dollar, so although a sterling/DMark deal may not appear to involve the US dollar at all, the interbank market will normally seek to lay off such a deal by doing two deals, one a dollar/sterling deal and the other a dollar/DMark deal. Clearly these laying off deals cannot be completed for settlement on a day when New York is closed and therefore the market does not conventionally quote even a DMark/sterling deal for settlement on a day when New York is closed. It is standard practice in the foreign exchange market to use the following conventions to fix the spot date for European currencies:

*a*: Where a currency is dealt against the US dollar such as French franc against US dollar, the spot date is usually fixed as the second working day forward in the country of the currency, provided that day is a business day in New York. If that day is not a business day in New York, the settlement takes place on the next succeeding day which is a business day in both centres. That is, assuming no French holidays, a deal done on Monday would normally be for settlement on Wednesday; but if Wednesday was a New York holiday, settlement would be on Thursday.

*b*: The same applies for deals between dollars and sterling, that is, the spot date is the second working day forward in London, provided that that date is a business day in New York.

*c*: Spot date for currencies other than the dollar dealt against sterling is fixed for the second working day forward in London, provided that that date is a business day both in the country of the relevant currency and New York.

*d*: For dealings of far eastern currencies, or Canadian dollars, against US dollars the same rules apply except that spot date is taken as the first working day forward rather than the second.

It will be seen from this that because of the existence of holidays in various centres, spot date can on occasion be as far away as a week in calendar time from the day on which the deal was done.

CONVENTIONAL QUOTATION OF SPOT FOREIGN EXCHANGE

On the London and other European foreign exchange markets (such as Frankfurt, Zurich, Paris, Amsterdam, etc.), foreign exchange rates are normally quoted as units of currency per US dollar. The main exception to this convention is sterling where the rate is expressed as US dollar per unit of the base currency. However, let us look at the usual case of say the DMark quoted against the dollar. A quote given to you by the bank may for instance be –

1·81 20/30

Like many other things in the foreign exchange market, this is a shorthand which is useful so long as you know the convention lying behind the figures. In the above quote the 'quoted currency' is DMark and the 'base' is the dollar.

The bank always refers to the quoted currency when saying 'buy' or 'sell'. For instance, the selling rate is the rate at which the bank sells the quoted currency against the base: the buying rate is the rate at which the bank buys the quoted currency. Secondly, the bank's selling rate is always quoted first and is always the lowest number.

These two facts can be remembered by the following simple rhyme –

> Sell low, buy high
> Hello, bye bye

This *aide mémoire* is useful because not only does the rhyme help to remember the principle, but also follows normal logic in that in the same way as 'hello' precedes 'bye bye', so does 'sell low' precede 'buy high'. Here the bank sells DMarks at 1·81 20, the bank buys DMarks at 1·81 30.

It may be useful at this point to dispose of some pieces of jargon which often serve to confuse in quoting these rates.

In the above example of 1·81 20/30 the '1', being the cents figure, is referred to as the 'big' figure: the 20 and 30, which are 100ths of a cent, are referred to as 'points', so in conversation the rate may be quoted to the customer as '20/30 on 1', or 'I make you 20/30 on a big figure of 1'. The gap between the selling price and the buying price of 10 points is the banker's turn and is referred to as the 'spread'. In conversation between market operators the 1·8 figure will be assumed to be known by everybody and will not usually be mentioned, except possibly in conclusion of the deal by way of confirmation.

Sterling is quoted for all centres as a price of US dollar per £. Here the dollar is considered to be the 'currency' being sold against a sterling base. Therefore a quote of 2·10 20/25 means that the bank is prepared to sell dollars at the rate of 2·10 20 and that the bank is prepared to buy dollars at the rate of 2·10 25. Here again the 'big' figure would be '0' and the points would be 20/25.

Rates are normally quoted verbally as 'one seventy twenty' not 'one point seven zero two zero'. It is a helpful practice when

writing exchange rates to leave a gap between the first two digits
and the second two digits, thus:

2·10 20

Certain other currencies are also quoted on the same convention
as sterling. Of these the most important are probably South
African rand and Australian dollars. That is, Australian dollars
are quoted as –

1·06 72/82 US dollars per Australian dollar

# 4    Forward Foreign Exchange

This market is possibly one of the least understood of all the areas of the international money markets. It is often viewed as mysterious, arcane, quite possibly dangerous and probably to be avoided. It has not helped that on a few widely publicised occasions it has been used as a medium of large scale speculation with disastrous results for the speculators. Most people using the market however are using it as a means to reduce or eliminate risks and this is its basic purpose. It is perhaps as if people were unwilling to purchase hammers because from time to time they are used as murder weapons. Whilst this is undoubtedly true, the murder clearly arises from abuse by the user rather than from any initiative by the hammer.

In order to explain how forward contracts work, it may be helpful to go back some 500 years and look at the origins of the technique, for even at that time the first international banking business was well under way in the Plain of Lombardy. It was conducted in the open air in the town squares by dealers sitting on benches. (As an aside, the Italian for bench is 'banco' and this is the origin of the fact that in many European languages the word for 'bench' is the same as the word for bank.) We will follow the situation of a man wishing to buy wine at the seasonal fair to be held over the state border. We will assume, too, that the currency in his home city is lira and the currency over the border is the thaler, or, as pronounced today, dollar.

In the first year our wine buyer decided to wait until the day of the fair and went to the money changers sitting on their banco to buy dollars with which to buy the wine. On this occasion the bankers said to him, 'It is a pity that you came today because if you had come a week ago the dollar would have been cheaper'.

So the second year, as the wine was being harvested, the man thought about the wine he would buy in the autumn and went to the money changer some weeks before the fair. He bought his dollars and put them on fixed deposit until the date of the fair. On the day of the fair he collected his deposit proceeds and went to buy the wine.

In the third year our wine buyer was becoming more ambitious. He found that he had quite a market for his wine in his home city but he did not have enough money to buy all the dollars in the middle of the summer and leave them on deposit until the day of the fair. So he borrowed the lire required from the banker and used the loan to buy the dollars and put the dollars on deposit as before.

This transaction had a number of effects:

1. He spent no money at all until the day of the fair.

2. His exchange rate was the rate between lire and dollars the day he made the transactions. He also received interest on the dollars and paid interest on the lire. So his total cost changed by the interest differential between the two currencies. That is, if the interest rate he paid on the lire was 8% per annum, and he received 4% per annum on his dollars and he dealt three months ahead of the date of the fair, it will have cost him 1%. That is –

$$(8\% - 4\%) \times \frac{3 \text{ months}}{12 \text{ months}} = 1\%$$

In this way he was able to cover his risk forward year after year with absolute certainty at a known cost and without anyone concerned with the transaction having to forecast future interest or exchange rates.

In most of Europe this was the process used until the twentieth century. Then during the depression years of the twenties and thirties several European countries introduced comprehensive Exchange Control regulations as defensive weapons in the prevailing climate of trade war and competitive devaluation. The object was usually to conserve the country's foreign exchange reserves and to control the flow of money across the exchanges. These regulations were usually intensified during the Second World War. The result is that in most of the countries of post-war Europe it has become illegal to do either the loan or the deposit, or the exchange deal, without prior permission. So the 'forward outright' deal was invented, one deal thus replacing three.

Today the economics of forward outright deals are precisely as they were for the wine grower, that is, the forward price is the spot price ruling on the day the deal is done plus the interest differential for the period concerned.

This story illustrates rather simply the flaw in the widespread belief that forward exchange rates represent some kind of best forecast of what the rate will actually be on the future date concerned. On the contrary, it is a straightforward calculation from three facts, all of which can be determined on the first day –

– the spot exchange date ruling on the day;
– the interest rate at which the customer borrows the sold currency;
– the interest rate at which the customer deposits the bought currency.

So it will be a matter of coincidence whether the exchange rate arrived at comes out the same as the spot rate on the future date. There is however normally some likelihood that the exchange rate will actually move in the direction shown by the calculation because currencies with high interest rates are often also those expected to depreciate. The reason for this is simply that without the attraction of higher interest rate no one would be willing to hold a currency which was expected to depreciate – as well illustrated by sterling in recent years. In practice though this is not always the case and even when it is, that depreciation may occur either much more slowly or much more quickly than the forward exchange rate calculation would suggest. In particular the forward rate is a notoriously bad predictor of spot exchange movements over the sort of short periods that are normally of interest to the corporate treasurer.

Despite this, various studies by economists have sought to show that for some major currencies a company consistently using the spot instead of the forward market would not have shown significant net overall losses. But this has only been true as an average over a period of many years and for certain currencies. For most companies, simply hoping to break even on a long run average basis will provide little consolation or justification for short term losses caused by leaving assets in a depreciating currency uncovered.

One natural consequence of this fact is that it will not usually pay a company to have a 100% consistent policy of covering all exchange exposure forward or, alternatively, a 100% consistent policy that the company will never cover anything forward. Some form of selective use of the market will be necessary to get the best results.

## Forward Foreign Exchange as Insurance

But companies must also consider the advantages they gain from the insurance aspects of forward cover. It may well be more important that a company should know precisely what its cash flow will be in terms of its home currency, even if this should also remove the chance of a possible speculative gain.

We have discussed in earlier chapters the rapid increase in the volatility of exchange rates. The risk inherent in taking foreign exchange positions, or in not forward covering known forward positions, has therefore continued to rise. Despite this, due to the way in which the cost of forward cover is calculated, based on interest differentials, the cost of covering the risk has not appreciably increased. So the forward exchange market is an insurance type market where the cost of cover does not relate in a very direct way to the scale of the risk covered and where the value for money in terms of risk covered per pound of premium spent has improved markedly over recent years.

Where a company, say in the USA, is due to receive a given sum of money in sterling in three months' time and is aware of this fact, if it does not cover the exchange risk forward, then it is speculating, or at least taking a calculated risk. This is not necessarily bad, but it is nevertheless the case. Since the company always has the possibility to sell the sterling forward, so as to receive a known amount in dollars in three months' time, if it chooses not to do that but to wait until the day on which the sterling arrives and then convert it to dollars, it should at least take this decision consciously and not simply by default. There are some companies which in the past have done forward contracts and have discovered, as inevitably they will from time to time, that had they not done the forward contract they would have got a better rate on the future day than the rate at which they did their forward deal. It is tempting to say that because the forward deal did not pay on that occasion, then maybe the company should not do forward deals in future.

However, it can be argued just as well that the same company no doubt insures its premises against fire. If the factory did not burn down during the year, the fire premium has been wasted and therefore maybe the company should not make the same mistake next year and so should stop insuring against fire.

For some reason it seems to be readily apparent to people that that would be a silly decision, but not also apparent that the equivalent decision on forward exchange cover is equally illogical. It is important that the insurance aspect of foreign exchange is valued for itself, leaving aside whether or not one might be making a profit in the short run out of the transaction. The value of this insurance against any future movement of exchange rate during the period covered, perhaps lies in the field of pricing, more accurate control of cash flow, budgeting and so on.

## Flexibility

Reverting to our US company in receipt of sterling three months hence, and looking at its position from the point of view of a market dealer, the market dealer will view the situation as being that he must do a deal some time within the next 90 days to sell the sterling either today or on the last day of the three months (more strictly, two days ahead of that date) or some day in between. The option does not arise at all of simply not doing the deal, the question is simply when. Viewed this way, our market operator has possibly 75 days or so to choose from and if he decides to wait a week, he has reduced his possible number of dealing days to 70. It will not usually be a good idea for our market operator to wait until the last day available to him and do the transaction then, because it is perfectly possible that the market might suffer some disturbance that day, causing perhaps a large but temporary shift in the market against him. Having left it so late, he cannot decide to leave it until tomorrow, but must deal that day however bad the rate is. Thus, if for some good reason a company decides not to cover forward, they should not then assume that they need do nothing until the spot date but should continually review the situation to see if they can deal on a day when the rate happens to favourable to them. Equally, any substantial adverse trend building up in the market will be apparent if they are keeping the situation under review, and they will be able to do a deal before the situation becomes even worse.

Before going on to consider other aspects of the use of foreign exchange deals, it may clarify the matter to set out a couple of typical uses of the forward foreign exchange deal.

### 1. UK IMPORTER OF FRENCH WINES

Here the importer has contracted to pay for wine at a price fixed in French francs. Let us assume that the wine is not due to be delivered until the autumn, and it is now only spring. Even at this stage price lists, advertising and many other matters must be prepared, and the importer may want to fix now the prices at which he will sell the wine to his customers in the winter season ahead.

These selling prices will be expressed in sterling. He therefore stands at risk that, when payment for the wine is due, the sterling cost may be greater than anticipated, with the result that his profit margin would be substantially reduced or even eliminated.

If this importer buys his French francs forward he will know with certainty the sum in sterling which he will have to pay out on the due date for the wine.

This in turn ensures that he is able to set his selling prices for wine as from the day he deals with his bankers and can be sure of the profit margin thus secured. Whatever happens to exchange rates in the meantime, he is insulated from those movements.

### 2. GERMAN EXPORTER OF MACHINERY TO SWEDEN

A German manufacturer of machinery has costs and overheads expressed in DMarks, but has agreed to price goods sold to Sweden in Swedish kronor for marketing reasons.

Consequently, he is at risk that the Swedish kronor due to him, when eventually received, may not provide sufficient DMarks to cover his costs and anticipated profit margin. However, if he sells his expected Swedish kronor receipts forward, he can fix the amount in DMarks that he will receive for his goods on the due date. This secures his profit margin and protects him against any adverse change in exchange rates in the interim.

## Option Date Contracts

It may be complained that these two examples are clear enough, but that many problems arise because in practice life is not that tidy. In particular it is rather unusual for the commercial firm involved in the import and export of physical goods to know with complete accuracy shipment dates and therefore payment dates. For many products, although an overall contract may exist for say 20,000 tons of a given commodity at a given price per ton, it is not known exactly what tonnage will arrive per shipment and therefore what the sum of money to be covered will turn out to be. So the company may be faced with a forward exchange risk where the date of the payment is not known with any accuracy and where, quite possibly, the amount of the payment will not be accurately known either.

The markets have however devised various solutions that at least partially handle this situation. Consider first the case where the company knows accurately the amount of the payment that it will have to make in the future, but does not know precisely when that payment will be required. The foreign exchange market offers a service in 'option forwards' which works as follows.

As discussed above, the normal foreign exchange contract is a contract to exchange two currencies on a future date at an agreed rate. The option contract extends this idea to allow the customer to call for settlement of the contract at two days' notice between any two dates that the customer agrees with the bank on the first day. Thus for instance the customer may contract to buy DMarks and sell dollars for settlement on any date between 5 April and 12 July and the bank will quote one rate which will be good for settlement on any day between and inclusive of those two dates.

It is up to the company to choose the two dates to suit the likely pattern of their payments. The closer together the two dates are – that is the shorter the option period – the finer price the bank will quote. This is because the bank must recognise that the company has the right under the contract to call for settlement on the worst day for the bank (and therefore the best day for the company) during the period of the option. The bank is therefore likely to price the deal on the worst exchange rate, from the company's point of view, existing for any date during the option period. The option applies, of course, only to the date of the settlement. Settlement must be made at some time during the period, at the latest on the last day.

Option contracts are normally used to cover whole months straddling the likely payment date, such as 'an option for the month of July' or for any other two dates that in the company's experience are likely to straddle the payment date. Many companies use option contracts as a matter of course when covering forward up to six months, using a narrow option period of seven days from start to finish. The purpose of this technique is to avoid having to renew a forward contract and extend it for a few days due to some administrative problem close to the due payment date causing a delay. Extending contracts in this way is normally rather expensive in terms of cost per day and it may be cheaper to take out an option period in the first place to allow for this type of delay. By using this technique a company may cover its foreign exchange exposure with certainty, even when the date is not known accurately.

It is normal practice for a company with an option contract to be able to use the option bit by bit. For instance a company having a $1 million contract against French francs on option for the month of June may wish to pay out $250,000 on 2 June, $200,000 on 18 June and so on until the $1 million contract is used up. It is not necessary to make one call for the whole amount on one date.

OVERLAPPING OPTIONS

There is a particular situation where these two techniques of option contracts and part calling option contracts can be used together to some effect. This is where a company has a sizeable expenditure or income in currency made up of a number of smaller sized transactions.

In the normal course of events these transactions are dealt with on what one might call an 'automatic' basis, the company instructing its bank to buy or sell currency only when the payment date arrives. Often in fact the company is unaware of the foreign exchange transaction, as it is done on its behalf by its bank. This method has four main disadvantages:
- the rate offered for each transaction will be poor, as the amount involved is small – perhaps $\frac{1}{4}$ to $\frac{1}{2}$% worse;
- there may be a separate bank commission or foreign exchange charge for each transaction;
- the company is totally exposed to exchange rate movements;
- currency is received or paid at a wide variety of exchange rates, which can unnecessarily complicate sales and purchase ledger accounting and reconciliation.

It is often practical to improve on this method, as follows:

1. Assess the monthly total income or expenditure in each currency. If it is not possible to do this on a month by month basis, as there is no certainty of cash flows, do it on a quarter by quarter basis.

2. Take out overlapping option contracts to cover the expected cash flows.

To take an example:

Widget Co. Ltd supplies spare parts for its products to Germany. It is paid in DMarks receiving various amounts, ranging from 6,000 DM to 50,000 DM at a time, throughout the month. The company predicts an overall inflow of DM for the three months January to March as shown below, although it cannot be confident of receiving more than 75% of the value in any one month.

|  | Predicted | 75% of value | 25% of value |
|---|---|---|---|
| January | 250,000 | 187,500 | |
| February | 170,000 | 127,500 | 207,500 |
| March | 410,000 | 307,500 | |

The company now takes out simultaneously four option contracts with its bankers:

| | |
|---|---|
| Sale between 1–31 January | DM187,500 |
| Sale between 1–28 February | DM127,500 |
| Sale between 1–31 March | DM307,500 |
| Sale between 1 Jan.–31 Mar. | DM207,500 |

The company arranges with its bankers that each DM receipt should be taken up against the month-at-a-time option until this is complete, and then should be taken up against the three month overlapping option. If, at the end of the month, the relevant month's contract is not fully taken up, the balance will be rolled forward to the next month. Any overall surplus is sold on the spot market. These instructions are carried out without reference back. At the end of the day, what has the company gained?

– it has covered its exchange risk;
– the overall rate it obtained for one large deal probably saved £300–£400 when compared with the poorer rate normally quoted on individual low value deals;
– sales accounting may well be simplified by the more uniform rates at which the income is converted.

**Extending a Forward Contract**

Often goods are delivered late and so the due payment date is delayed. In these circumstances foreign exchange contracts may be extended to conform to the new settlement date.

As a matter of procedure, the bank may require that the original contract be settled and a new one taken out for the period of the extension, rather than 'rolling the old contract forward'.

Suppose a company sells DM1 million forward against sterling when the rates are:

| | | |
|---|---|---|
| Spot | 4·26 | April |
| 3 months fwd | 4·14 | July |

This contract will yield

$$\frac{1,000,000}{4\cdot14} = £241,546$$

on maturity in July. After two months, in June, it becomes apparent that payment of the DMarks will be delayed until August, so the customer asks to extend the contract. At this time the existing contract has one month to run and the market rates are now:

| | | |
|---|---|---|
| Spot | 3·98 | June |
| 1 month | 3·93 | July |
| 2 months | 3·89 | August |
| 3 months | 3·86 | September |

The bank will now sell the DMarks back to the customer at the new outright rate to July i.e. 3·93 and will require

$$\frac{1,000,000}{3\cdot93} = £254,453 \text{ in settlement.}$$

This sum of money is provided as to £241,546 from the maturing proceeds of the original contract, and the shortfall of £12,907 must be paid in by the customer at the same date.

A new contract is now taken out to the August date, that is, two months outright. The rate is 3·89 and so will yield

$$\frac{1,000,000}{3\cdot89} = £257,069 \text{ on maturity.}$$

The customer's cash flow thus becomes:

| | |
|---|---|
| Paid out in July | £12,907 |
| Received in August | £257,069 |
| Net | £244,162 |

The alternative, 'rolling the old contract forward' works as follows. It can be argued that since at current market rates the premium for extension amounts to 4 pfennig $(3\cdot93-3\cdot89)$ it would be simpler to extend the existing contract merely by adjusting the original rate by 4 pfennig. That is, for settlement in August the rate would be the original rate less the current premium, i.e. $4\cdot14-\cdot04=4\cdot10$. Sterling proceeds then become

$$\frac{1,000,000}{4\cdot10}=£243,902$$

which is more or less the same amount as before and avoids the complications of the intermediate settlement in July. Whilst this is often done, especially where the amount involved or the time difference is small, the method is inherently inaccurate and can give substantially incorrect answers at times.

But, from the bank's point of view, the main objection is that if the two stage settlement is not used then the bank is financing the company's loss at zero interest rate for the period of the extension. Further, the rollover technique postpones the realisation of loss in the company's books and may not be acceptable to either the company's bankers or its auditors for this reason. In theory of course the bank could allow for the interest cost of rolling the old contract by allowing for this in calculating the extension rate. In this example the bank might forego two stage settlement and make a single settlement of £244,000 in August. This would imply that the bank would otherwise expect to earn an extra £162 interest on the £12,907 had they lent it for the intervening month at say 15% per annum.

$$£12,907\times\frac{1}{12}\times\frac{15}{100}=£161\cdot3$$

**Value Dates for Forward Exchange Dealing**

Value date is spot date appropriate to the dealing date determined as outlined earlier plus the fixed period (1 month, etc.). If on the date arrived at one or both of the dealing centres are closed, value date is the next day on which both centres are open.

*Example 1*
Dealing dollar sterling for 1 month forward

|  |  | London | New York |
|---|---|---|---|
| Dealing date | Mon 7 Mar | OPEN | OPEN |
|  | Tue 8 Mar | OPEN | OPEN |
| Spot date | Wed 9 Mar | OPEN | OPEN |
| Spot + 1 month | Sat 9 Apr | HOLIDAY | HOLIDAY |
|  | Mon 11 Apr | HOLIDAY | OPEN |
| 1 Month value date | Tue 12 Apr | OPEN | OPEN |

*Example 2*
Dealing French francs per dollar 6 months forward

|  |  | Paris | London | New York |
|---|---|---|---|---|
| Dealing date | Mon 7 Mar | HOLIDAY | OPEN | OPEN |
|  | Tue 8 Mar | HOLIDAY | OPEN | OPEN |
|  | Wed 9 Mar | OPEN | OPEN | OPEN |
| Spot date | Thu 10 Mar | OPEN | OPEN | OPEN |
| Spot + 6 months | Sat 10 Sept | HOLIDAY | HOLIDAY | HOLIDAY |
| 6 month value date | Mon 12 Sept | OPEN | HOLIDAY | OPEN |

*Exception 1: End-End Rule*
If spot date is the last possible spot date for the month, then the value date for fixed periods forward is the last day in the month when both dealing centres are open.

*Example 3*
Dealing forward dollar sterling

|  |  | London | New York |
|---|---|---|---|
| Dealing date | Wed 24 Nov | OPEN | HOLIDAY |
|  | Thu 25 Nov | OPEN | OPEN |
| Spot date | Fri 26 Nov | OPEN | OPEN |
|  | Mon 29 Nov | HOLIDAY | OPEN |
|  | Tue 30 Nov | OPEN | HOLIDAY |
| 1 Month value date | Fri 31 Dec | OPEN | OPEN |
| 3 Month value date | Mon 28 Feb | OPEN | OPEN |
| 6 Month value date | Mon 30 May | OPEN | OPEN |
|  | Tue 31 May | OPEN | HOLIDAY |

*Exception 2: Months Rule* (Variation on End-End Rule)
If holidays etc. were to cause a forward value to go over a month
end, then the forward value date is fixed as the last day of the month
when both dealing centres are open so that the period does not
extend into the following calendar month.

*Example 4*
Dealing forward dollar sterling

|  |  | London | New York |
|---|---|---|---|
| Dealing date | Mon 24 Jan | OPEN | OPEN |
|  | Tue 25 Jan | OPEN | HOLIDAY |
| Spot date | Wed 26 Jan | OPEN | OPEN |
|  | Thu 27 Jan | OPEN | OPEN |
|  | Fri 28 Jan | OPEN | OPEN |
|  | Mon 31 Jan | OPEN | OPEN |
| 1 Month value date | Fri 25 Feb | OPEN | OPEN |
| Spot + 1 month | Sat 26 Feb | HOLIDAY | HOLIDAY |
| New York closed | Mon 28 Feb | OPEN | HOLIDAY |
| Spot + 2 months | Sat 26 Mar | HOLIDAY | HOLIDAY |
| 2 Month value date | Mon 28 Mar | OPEN | OPEN |
|  | Tue 29 Mar | OPEN | OPEN |
| 3 Month value date | Tue 26 Apr | OPEN | OPEN |

*Note*
In this example, Fri 25 Feb would be the 1 month value
date for all of the following spot dates:

|  |  |
|---|---|
| Tue | 25 Jan |
| Wed | 26 Jan |
| Thu | 27 Jan |
| Fri | 28 Jan |
| Mon | 31 Jan |

Whilst the value date would be the same for all these
dealing dates, the exchange rate would not, as the number
of days premium would differ for each starting date and of
course spot rate could be different on each dealing day
too.

## Conventional Quotation of Forward Foreign Exchange

*a: Outright Quote*
The 'Outright Quote' is simply the exchange rate that will apply to
sell or buy the currency against the reference currency, usually the

dollars, on the future date. It is quoted on the same convention as the spot rate thus:

DM/$ = 1·81 20/30 spot

similarly

DM/$ = 1·80 30/45 Outright for settlement on 1 July.

### b: Premium Quote

There is also a second more shorthand basis of quoting in which the forward premium, being defined as the difference between the spot price and the forward price, is quoted by itself. For instance, if our spot price was still 1·81 20/30, the forward premium would be expressed as 90/85 points.

1·80 30/45 = 1·81 20/30 − 90/85

Outright Price = Spot Price − Premium

Negative premiums are termed discounts. A currency having a lower interest rate than the dollar stands at a premium against the dollar, being more expensive forward than spot; a currency having a higher interest rate than the dollar stands at a discount against the dollar.

Strictly a currency at a discount should be quoted as:

+70/+85

In practice plus and minus signs are usually omitted because the sign is obvious from the following rule:

Bigger figure first = currency at a premium
Smaller figure first = currency at a discount

here    90/85    indicates premium
        70/85    indicates discount

This convention is helpful to market operators because this forward premium tends to be a reasonably static figure in the market, whereas the spot price may be rather volatile. Further, as discussed earlier, the forward premium tends to move in the market on different considerations than the spot price and it is helpful to keep the two factors that made the outright price, that is the spot price and the premium, separate.

### c: Premium Quote for Australian dollars, etc.

As mentioned in the previous chapter some currencies such as South African rand and Australian dollars are quoted as US dollars per Australian dollar, etc. This must be borne in mind when interpreting premium quotes in these currencies. For example, a forward premium quote for Australian dollars of 15/12 means US dollars at a premium versus Australian, or Australian dollars at a *discount* versus the US dollar.

### d: *Interest Calculation*

It will be seen from the arguments earlier in this chapter that the premium represents solely the interest differentials in the currencies. In a very approximate manner the interest differential in the currencies can be calculated by the following relationship:

$$\text{Interest differential \% per annum} = \frac{\text{Points per annum of premium}}{100 \times \text{spot rate}}$$

Here, assuming our premium of 90/85 to relate to a three month premium and taking the middle rate of $87\frac{1}{2}$ we get

$$\text{Interest differential} = \frac{87\frac{1}{2} \times \frac{12}{3}\%}{100 \times 1 \cdot 8125}$$

$$= 1 \cdot 93\% \text{ per annum}$$

So, if three month dollars are at 9%, three month DMarks will be at 7% approximately. (For a more exact version of this calculation see Chapter 5.)

# 5 Funding Swaps or Interest Arbitrage

## Swap Deals

We saw in the chapter about forward foreign exchange how the difference between the forward price and the spot price for a currency could usefully be expressed directly as a premium e.g. 90/85. This quote given by a bank indicates that it will buy DMarks spot and sell them forward for a premium of 90 points. Spot currency is being swapped for future currency. In the jargon they would say, 'We buy and sell the DMark for 90 points our favour'. The 90 points that the bank is gaining on the deal will be sufficient to compensate the bank for the lower interest rate it will receive on the DMarks.

Such swap deals are a frequent type of market transaction. Because the same amount of currency is bought as is sold, swap deals create no direct exposure to moves in the spot rate. One major use of the swap deal is the 'funding swap', or 'interest arbitrage' deal.

## Interest Arbitrage

We have already discussed the fact that the forward premium is derived from the interest differential between two currencies. This idea will now be used in reverse – to calculate interest rates.

Supposing a bank wishes to lend a customer $1 million worth of DMarks for three months but at the time can only borrow three month dollars, it can solve its problem by the following route –

  *a*: borrow three month dollars at say 9%;

  *b*: use the dollars to buy DMarks spot;

  *c*: lend the DMarks to the customer for the three months;

*d*: anticipating the customer's repayment of the DMarks, on the three month date, sell those DMarks forward to provide the dollars to repay the dollars borrowed.

In this way the bank is able to provide DMarks by borrowing dollars without any currency exposure to itself. Deals (a) (b) and (d) taken together are precisely equivalent to borrowing DMarks. Further, instead of buying the DMarks on the first date and selling them on the far date as two separate transactions, the dealer would simply do a swap deal and receive the premium. This reduces his exercise to three deals: borrow dollars, do the swap, lend the DMarks.

It will perhaps be helpful to go through the arithmetic for a specific case to illustrate the mechanism and also the rate calculations involved.

*Example*, Method 1

Data:   spot price                    1·81 20/30
        period                        91 days
        forward premium               90/85
        interest rate on dollars  9% per annum

Require: Rate at which bank can lend three month DMarks by borrowing dollars and doing a 'funding swap'.

Calculation:

*a*: borrow $1 million

$$\text{cost of interest} = \$9\% \times \frac{91}{360} \times 1{,}000{,}000$$

$$= \$22{,}750 \qquad (see\ note\ i)$$

*b*: receive on the swap 85 points (or ·0085 DMarks per dollar) on the *maturing* amount of $1,022,750 which is worth (*see note ii*)

DM ·0085 × 1,022,750
 = DM 8,693

$$= \$\ \frac{8{,}693}{1{\cdot}8125} = \$4{,}796$$

*c*: net cost of funds = $22,750 − $4,796
                       = $17,954

$$\text{Expressed as an interest rate} = \frac{17,954}{1,000,000} \times \frac{360}{91}$$

$$= 7 \cdot 103\%$$

This is the effective cost of the DMarks.

*Notes*:

i   All Eurocurrency market calculations assume a convention of a 360 day year.

ii  It may be wondered why the premium of 85 (bank sells spot and buys forward) rather than 90 (bank buys spot and sells forward), is used in the calculation since here the bank does buy DMarks spot and sell them forward. The reason is that the bank is here acting as a customer itself, perhaps having to do this deal at the market price with, say, ABC Bank. In doing this it will have to take the price at which *ABC Bank sells* spot and buys forward, i.e. 85 points rather than 90.

*Example*, Method 2
This calculation can be done more quickly by use of a formula:

$$R_L = R_B - \frac{P \times 3 \cdot 6}{DS}\left(1 + \frac{R_B D}{36,000}\right)$$

where

$R_L$ = Rate on currency lent, %
$R_B$ = Rate on currency borrowed, %
$P$ = Premium for forward purchase, points
$S$ = Middle spot price
$D$ = No. of days in period

here:

$R_B = 9\%$
$P = 85$ points
$S = 1 \cdot 81\ 25$ DMarks/dollar
$D = 91$ days

So,

$$R_L = 9 - \frac{85 \times 3 \cdot 6}{91 \times 1 \cdot 8125}\left(1 + \frac{9 \times 91}{36,000}\right)$$
$$= 9 - 1 \cdot 8552 \, (1 \cdot 02275)$$
$$= 9 - 1 \cdot 8974$$
$$= 7 \cdot 103\%$$

*Example*, Method 3

Lastly, there is the quick (but only approximate) method mentioned in Chapter 4:

$$\text{Interest differential} = \frac{C}{S}$$

where

$C$ = middle premium in cents per annum

$S$ = middle spot price

here:

$$C = 0 \cdot 875 \times \frac{12 \text{ months}}{3 \text{ months}} = 3 \cdot 5 \, \text{¢/annum}$$

$S = 1 \cdot 81 \, 25$ DMarks/dollar

$$\text{Approx. interest differential} = \frac{3 \cdot 5}{1 \cdot 8125} = 1 \cdot 931$$

$$\text{Approx. DMark interest rate} = 9 - 1 \cdot 931 = 7 \cdot 07\%$$

The rate at which DMarks can be produced in this manner using the forward DMark market and the Eurodollar market, is very closely identical to the Euro DMark rate. Where it is not, the action of the market tends to put it back into line in a very short time, so the existence of the large and reasonably stable Eurodollar market, together with the existence of reasonably reliable forward markets, enables the market to construct deposit and lending rates for any major currency. This provides the underlying basis for deposit rates quoted in London and other centres for deposit and loan transactions in these currencies.

**The Interest Rate Trap**

It should be borne in mind that it follows from the structure of the rates that borrowing in a low interest rate currency, or placing deposits in a high interest rate currency, may not necessarily be a good thing, since all currencies provide the same expected yield in dollars after allowing for the forward premium. A classic example of this interest rate trap is provided by the very large scale borrowings of Swiss francs which many corporations made during the late 60s and early 70s because of the very low interest rate on Swiss francs. These have resulted in extremely high capital losses to the companies concerned due to the fact that the Swiss franc appreciated against the US dollar by amounts of up to 25%, depending on the dates involved. The converse – trying to make a little more money on the interest rate – is illustrated by the following example which in fact actually happened a few years ago.

This particular example arises from the question of a Norwegian investor asking why it was such a good idea to be putting money on deposit in London at $6\frac{3}{8}\%$ when he could get $8\frac{1}{4}\%$ in Norway. Looking a little more closely at this innocent sounding proposition and rephrasing it somewhat, the question is, 'Is it better to put US dollars on deposit in London at $6\frac{3}{8}\%$ or to put Norwegian kroner on deposit at $8\frac{1}{4}\%$?'. In order to answer the question we first need to know a little bit more about it. For instance, after the three month period of the deposit will the money be used to make a payment in Norway, or will it be used to make a payment somewhere else in US dollars? Apart from anything else, it is only prudent to keep the money in the currency in which it is going to be spent if that is possible. In this case the eventual expenditure was going to be in US dollars, but still there was that temptation to keep the money in Norwegian kroner for the sake of the 2% differential that existed. The course of events was as follows.

*Interest Rate Trap – 14 May 1975*
Situation:
> Company has $1 million for placement for three months. It has payments to make in US dollars at the end of this period. Should they place dollars on deposit at $6\frac{3}{8}\%$ or convert to Norwegian kroner and place those on deposit at the better rate of $8\frac{1}{4}\%$?

Outcome:

   *a*: $1 million dollars placed on deposit for three months yields $1,015,937 at maturity, or

   *b*: on 14 May dollars could be converted to Norwegian kroner at 4·85 50. So after three months the company receives:

| | | |
|---|---|---|
| the principal | Nkr | 4,855,000 |
| +interest | | 100,134 |
| | Nkr | 4,955,134 |

But after the three months was over, on 14 August 1975, the exchange rate had moved to Nkr/$ = 5·46 00 so the proceeds amounted to –

$$\frac{\$4,955,134}{5\cdot46\,00} = \$907,534$$

Difference relative to option (a) $108,403

It will be seen that, because of the subsequent fall of the Norwegian krone relative to the dollar during the three months, the company involved would have lost out by $108,403 representing a 43% per annum loss – and all incurred for the sake of trying to make 2%!

In recent years the movements in exchange rates have usually considerably exceeded any likely interest rate differential. The conclusion follows that interest rate should not have been an important criterion in making the currency choice, selecting the currency for its relevance to the company's anticipated cash flow or for its likely exchange market performance is overwhelmingly important.

## Feedback

It may be complained that if the forward exchange price is fixed from the interest rates in the first place, it is rather difficult to then use those prices to fix the interest rates – who is fooling who? The fact of the matter is more complicated than it might seem because there is a feedback between spot exchange rates, forward exchange rates and interest rates of a very complex nature.

For instance, if an economy is seen to be starting to expand, there will be a tendency for interest rates to go up as the economy takes up credit from the banking system. The higher yield now available from this currency will tend to make it more attractive to hold and also improved prospects for that country tend to push the spot rate up independently. The market will then look at the forward outright prices and see if they still look reasonable. If the market feels that they don't, then they may modify the forward premium, which in turn will react back on interest rates. So these three factors are continually in a state of readjustment to each other and at any one time one element can be the moving force in the market causing the others to react.

# 6 Using Currency Deposit Markets

## The Eurodollar Market

Many people have complained that the 'Eurodollar Market' is a particularly unhelpful name. Originally the Eurodollar was any dollar bank account that was owned by other than a US resident. The term 'Euro' was attached to the dollar to indicate the probable ownership of the dollar in question to be European rather than North American. The basic fact is that a Eurodollar is a dollar is a dollar. Ignoring entirely why it was necessary to invent a new word at all, this new word then went on to be used to mean other things too. Today Eurodollar still means any dollars not owned by a US citizen. Many of these will be owned and traded outside European centres, such as Bahrain or Singapore (where it may be called an Asian dollar). Even more confusing is the common journalistic practice of calling all those markets of non-resident funds, whether in dollars or not, by the casual title 'The Eurodollar Market'. Some, rather more accurately, use the term 'Eurocurrency market' to refer to all the international loan and deposit markets that exist for dollars, DMarks, sterling, French francs, Swiss francs, guilders and indeed many other currencies.

These markets which have grown up in the last fifteen years or so from practically nothing, represent a major source of finance for international borrowers. The size of the market was estimated to be some $900 billion in 1980, about 70% of which was in US dollars. Dollars deposited in London on the Eurodollar market by Arab investors may be on loan to finance a new paper mill in Canada, or an engineering works in France. The intermediaries in this market are of course the banks and the principal centre of the market remains London, which accounts alone for nearly half of world turnover in the Eurodollar markets.

## Banking Services

All company treasurers are familiar with the operation of their company's bank accounts in their home currency. As international business becomes more complex it is becoming increasingly useful to maintain banking accounts in foreign currencies. As these markets have expanded and developed over the last fifteen years or so, several different forms of currency banking services have become available to the corporate treasurer.

This chapter describes the main currency banking services presently available; not all international banks will offer all of them and some may offer other special services not described here. The availability of these services to particular companies is subject to the Exchange Control rules of their country of incorporation. These rules can be complex and are altered from time to time. No Exchange Control considerations arise for companies based in North America, the United Kingdom, West Germany or Switzerland.

## Deposits on Short Notice

These accounts are available for the deposit of most major currencies on a two day notice or seven day notice basis. For US dollars, accounts are also available on a call basis whereby 'value today' is applied to payments over the account. That is, funds received today start to earn interest as from today.

Most banks require some minimum balance before interest is payable and some make charges for items passing over the account. There is no such thing as 'the market rate' for notice money as no interbank wholesale market has yet developed on a notice basis; each bank fixes its own rate in relation to its own funding situation and competitor's quotes. Rates of interest paid are of course changed from time to time and banks usually give their customers two days' notice of such rate changes.

Certain banks offer a multicurrency cheque book service for use in conjunction with a notice account and this can make sense for companies with a large number of small transactions arising in, perhaps, several currencies. For this purpose a company can draw cheques on a currency account in any major currency in which it is required to make payments. Any foreign exchange transactions that may be necessary are handled when the cheques are cleared, so that the customer is not restricted to drawing cheques only in the currencies he holds. This makes payment of small amounts quick and reliable and avoids cumbersome procedures.

Nearly all companies maintaining accounts in currencies keep at least one notice account. The reasons are the traditional ones of ease and flexibility of operation and, of course, the need for liquidity. A particular advantage of a currency notice account is that it can allow a company with a two-way currency cash flow largely to match receipts and payments in currency whilst keeping temporary surpluses on the account. Where this matching can be done, exchange risks are directly set off and thus eliminated.

### Fixed, or 'Time', Deposits

A better return is usually obtainable on fixed deposits, and normally the longer the deposit the higher the rate paid. There is a very large and well established wholesale interbank market in fixed deposits for the principal currencies and so 'the market rate for three month Dutch guilders' has a genuine meaning. The interbank market normally trades in multiples of $1 million or its currency equivalent and deposits of smaller amounts will not necessarily attract the same rate of interest. Periods quoted range from a few days up to one year for most currencies with quotes for longer periods being available only in the major three or four Eurocurrencies – the US dollar, DMark, Swiss franc and Dutch guilder.

### US Dollar Certificates of Deposit

A special market has grown up in London in 'US Dollar Certificates of Deposit'. Some 130 London banks form the 'Primary Market' and they issue their certificates against dollars deposited. The customer receives a bearer certificate stating that a given sum of money has been deposited with their bankers and will be repaid with interest to bearer at maturity. CDs are issued for sums of $25,000 and over for fixed periods of one month upwards. The customer has the option to hold the certificate until maturity or to sell it on the secondary market for cash at any time during its life at current market rates. The Certificate itself may not be sent outside the United Kingdom and is normally held by the issuing bank on behalf of the customer until required either for sale or at maturity. In this way a company can take advantage of the higher interest rates prevailing for fixed periods without giving up liquidity, making CD's a very popular form of deposit for the larger company. The limitation is that these arrangements are only available for US dollars.

Some companies have taken this a step further and invest in CDs as an investment medium when they expect interest rates to fall, in the expectation of making a capital gain on the resale of the CD. (As would be the case in the Example shown below.)

The secondary market is provided either by repurchase by the issuing bank or by the fourteen member firms of the International CD Market Association made up of certain specialist houses together with the London Discount Houses.

## CD REPURCHASE VALUE

In the secondary market, dollar CDs are quoted on a yield to maturity basis using the 'present value' method of calculation. When outstanding CDs are traded the following information must be supplied.

1. The date of issue.

2. The maturity date.

3. The rate of interest stated on the CD (or issue rate).

4. The nominal amount (or face value) of the CD.

Net proceeds can then be calculated using the following formula:

Net proceeds =

$$\text{nominal amount} \times \frac{(100 \times 360) + (\text{issue rate} \times \text{original life in days})}{(100 \times 360) + (\text{traded rate} \times \text{remaining life})}$$

as shown in the following example.

*Example*
A CD for US $1 million having a total life of 184 days and bearing interest at $7\frac{1}{8}\%$ is sold after 24 days at $6\frac{15}{16}\%$. The CD has 160 days to run to maturity:

$$\text{Proceeds} = \$1,000,000 \times \frac{36,000 + (7\tfrac{1}{8} \times 184)}{36,000 + (6\tfrac{15}{16} \times 160)}$$
$$= \$1,005,416 \cdot 33$$

## Difficulties

In all these types of deposit account the golden rule must be to keep the funds in the currency in which they are most likely to be required for future expenditure. The possible adverse consequences of depositing in a different currency solely to take advantage of a higher interest rate were discussed in Chapter 5.

Unfortunately, although this sounds simple enough it may not always be that straightforward. For instance:

 *a*: There may be no international deposit market in the currency concerned, or

 *b*: At the time the initial deposit has to be made, the currency of expenditure may not yet be known. Quite possibly no expenditure is immediately in prospect at all and there is an investment situation, or

 *c*: The company may have a cash flow in very many currencies so that the operation of accounts in all of them would be prohibitively cumbersome.

Let us look at these problems in turn.

NO MARKET

Although the Eurocurrency market is very large it is heavily concentrated in relatively few currencies. The extent of this concentration is not always realised. Estimates of the proportion of the market represented by each currency vary but within a percent or two the breakdown was approximately as follows in 1979:

| Currency | % of total |
|----------|------------|
| US dollars | 70 |
| DMark | 17 |
| Swiss franc | $6\frac{1}{2}$ |
| French franc | 2 |
| Sterling | $1\frac{1}{2}$ |
| Dutch guilder | $1\frac{1}{2}$ |
| All others* | $1\frac{1}{2}$ |
| Total | 100 |

* Within this category the most significant currencies are probably yen, Belgian francs, Canadian dollars, Italian lire, Swedish kronor, Norwegian kroner. Even including these there are only twelve currencies thus far, making up some 99% of the total market.

The effect of this concentration is to restrict the ability of banks to match transactions in the less active currencies. In turn they may be reluctant to quote or will require larger margins in these currencies than when quoting for the 'top 12'.

This difficulty does not invalidate the general principle of trying to place funds in the currency of eventual expenditure as an aim but it must be appreciated that of the 140 or so currencies of the Western World only about 30 have a functioning international deposit market. A further consideration is that many of these other currencies are from the less developed countries of the world and tend to be very weak relative to those of the industrial countries, often undergoing repeated devaluations (e.g. in South America). For this reason it would usually be unwise to place deposits in such currencies even if a market came to be developed.

In this situation the usual solution is to place the funds in US dollars – being the largest, and therefore most competitive market and being a currency likely to be stronger than the currency of eventual expenditure.

CURRENCY OF EXPENDITURE NOT KNOWN

It can arise that a company has, say, dollars for investment for three months (at the end of which time the funds will be needed to pay suppliers) but that the currency of the payments will not be known until one month from now. At least three possible courses of action suggest themselves:

1. As mentioned above, usually a longer fixed deposit earns a higher rate of interest than a shorter period. So it may look a good idea to place dollars on deposit for three months to earn the best yield. When the deposit matures these funds are used to purchase the currency required on a spot basis, or

2. Place dollars on deposit for one month. Convert to the currency required (say Swiss francs) and place a new Swiss franc deposit for two months. When this deposit matures pay the supplier, or

3. Place dollars on deposit for three months. After one month take out a forward purchase contract to buy Swiss francs and sell dollars for settlement on the date the deposit matures. The forward contract is satisfied by the maturing deposit proceeds in dollars and delivers the Swiss franc countervalue to the depositor instead.

Of these alternatives method (1) leaves the currency risk uncovered for two months and is therefore to be avoided. Method (2) is workable enough and does cover the risk adequately but method (3) will nearly always yield more. This is because, unless interest rates are in a period of rapid rise, a three month deposit will usually yield more than a one month deposit plus a two month deposit.

This mechanism enables an existing deposit to continue to run undisturbed whilst fixing the exchange rate at which the maturity proceeds will be converted into the required currency. The technique is also widely used by firms who have substantial funds on short term deposit, perhaps pending future capital expenditure. Where there are several possible suppliers in different countries and the eventual contract currency may be impossible to know, the treasurer's aim is usually to try and conserve the value of the funds as well as possible in the meanwhile.

Here, the funds may be invested in a series of fixed deposits in various currencies – probably those thought most likely to be used in the contract. If, during the life of the deposits, it either becomes apparent that one of the currencies in which the funds are invested is likely to become weaker because of some new development, or the contract currency becomes agreed, then forward contracts can be taken out which will have the effect of converting the existing deposits into the currency required on maturity without disturbing the deposits.

Some insurance companies face a related problem. For instance, the company may receive a dollar premium to insure a ship. The ship then is involved in a collision with a French vessel off the French coast, and is towed by a Dutch tug to a Belgian port for repair. The claim may arise in French francs, Belgian francs and Dutch guilders. If all the premiums received are invested in dollars then the sufficiency of the funds depends upon the recent course of the dollar versus the continental currencies. An insurance company is therefore likely to invest its funds in a range of currencies corresponding to its experience of the currency mix of claims, thereby spreading, at least on an average basis, the currency risk. But special problems arise when the number of currencies involved becomes very large and this we turn to next.

## MANAGING CASH FLOW IN MANY CURRENCIES

There are currently somewhat over 140 currencies in use in the Western World. Some companies with a very widespread international business may find themselves trying to manage exposures in anything up to 100 currencies. Bearing in mind the narrow, or non-existent market for a great many of the minor currencies and the sheer administrative problem of trying to handle a problem of this size, it is necessary to find some basis of simplification. Such simplification is bound to involve a degree of inaccuracy but this disadvantage is often outweighed by the greater ease with which the nature of the problem can then be understood. One way to approach this simplification is to classify currencies into groups. The argument runs as follows.

Firstly, the principal relationship on which all world foreign exchange rates are based has become the $/DM rate. For this reason the $/DM rate is often referred to as 'the pivotal rate'. This idea is carried forward into the diagram below which shows these two currencies balanced in the pans of the scale. All the other major currencies in the world are then assumed to be influenced to a greater or lesser extent by the dollar or DMark, or both.

The arrows linking the currencies on the diagram are drawn on the convention that the currency at the head of the arrow is influenced by the currency at the tail of the arrow, that is to say the

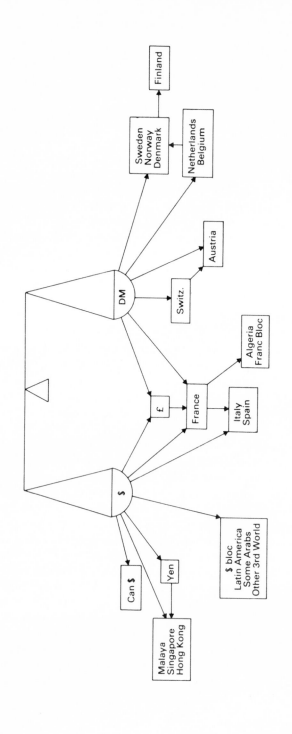

rate for sterling is determined principally by consideration of its level relative to the dollar and relative to the DMark. During the sixties and early seventies sterling has at times moved in line with the dollar, but at other times – when the $/DM rate was changing rapidly – sterling would follow an intermediate path, so that if the dollar rose 1% against the DMark, sterling would fall by $\frac{1}{2}$% against the dollar and rise by $\frac{1}{2}$% against the DMark. When it became necessary to allow sterling to fall in the market the extent of the fall was normally evaluated relative to the dollar or the DMark, or some weighted average of the two reflecting the UK trading pattern. Similarly the French franc probably has to take into account the level of sterling and the DMark, and the dollar, and in the past has tended to travel a path intermediate between the experience of those three currencies.

Within Europe a number of major currencies are linked together under the European Monetary System agreements, more commonly known as 'The Snake' – see Appendix A. Membership of the Snake has changed frequently since the beginnings of the system in 1972. For example, for most of the period France was a member, but the franc's tendency to follow the dollar and sterling to some extent, both of which have been consistently weaker than today's Snake currencies, has forced France to withdraw from time to time. Under the terms of the Snake arrangements, the members agree that their currencies shall not move relative to each other by more than $2\frac{1}{4}$% and that their respective Central Banks shall restrict movements to within this range by direct market intervention. Parities within the Snake have been adjusted from time to time but when they are, they are quoted as adjustments relative to the DMark.

Many currencies of the former French territories of West Africa are party to an agreement known as the Franc Bloc, whereby they maintain an agreed relationship between their own currency and the French franc. Similarly, many currencies of Latin America publish an exchange rate against the US dollar without too much regard to value relative to other currencies. This does not mean that such currencies are fixed relative to the dollar other than in the very short term. Some Latin American countries have had frequent and large devaluations against the dollar.

In the last ten years, when individual currencies have experienced substantial movements, some countries which previously fixed the value of their currency against only one of the major world currencies, usually dollars or sterling, have elected to base the value of their currency on a weighted average formula, usually calculated on the value of the currencies in which they have to pay for imports. Examples of this arrangement are Kuwait, Australia, New Zealand, South Africa, Nigeria and Tunisia. The result of this is that such countries frequently publish new guide rates for their own currency versus the US dollar, the adjustment necessary being designed to keep their own unit stable in terms of their chosen 'currency basket'.

Some countries have decided not to calculate their own currency basket but instead to use the IMF currency basket, the SDR – see Appendix B.

*Approximating the Risk*
The result of these arrangements, whereby many countries relate their currency to the dollar, the French franc, sterling or the DMark, or mixtures of these, is that it is possible to approximate a currency exposure arising in very many currencies by maintaining banking accounts in rather few. For most practical purposes worldwide, risk can be approximated by using seven currencies, possibly supplemented by the SDR. The usual seven chosen are dollars, DMarks, sterling and the currencies of Netherlands, Norway, France and Japan; without too much loss of accuracy this list can be reduced further by dropping Netherlands, Norway and SDR.

A possible way to group currencies is listed on pages 49–50. It is not complete or definitive – there are many other ways to group them which would probably work just as well.

1. DOLLAR GROUP

Afghanistan
Argentina
Bahamas
Barbados
Bolivia
Botswana
Brazil
Burundi
Canada
Chile
Republic of China
Colombia
Costa Rica
Dominican
   Republic
Ecuador
Egypt
El Salvador
Ethiopia
Fiji
Ghana
Guatemala
Guinea

Haiti
Honduras
Indonesia
Iraq
Israel
Jamaica
Kenya
Korea
Laos
Lesotho
Liberia
Libyan Arab
   Republic
Mexico
Nepal
Nicaragua
Oman
Pakistan
Panama
Paraguay
Philippines
Peru
Romania

Rwanda
Somalia
Sudan
Syrian Arab
   Republic
Tanzania
Thailand
Uganda
Uruguay
Venezuela
Viet Nam
Western Samoa
People's Dem.
   Republic of
   Yemen
Yemen Arab
   Republic
Zaire
Zambia

2. DEUTSCHE MARK GROUP

Austria                Switzerland

3. STERLING GROUP

Bangladesh
The Gambia
Guyana
India

Ireland
Mauritius
Sierra Leone

Sri Lanka
Trinidad and
   Tobago

4. FRENCH FRANC GROUP

Algeria
Cameroon
Central African
   Republic
Chad
People's Republic
   of the Congo

Dahomey
Gabon
Italy
Ivory Coast
Malagasy Republic
Mali

Niger
Portugal
Senegal
Spain
Togo
Upper Volta

5.   YEN GROUP

| Hong Kong | Malaysia | Singapore |
|---|---|---|

6.   GUILDER GROUP

| Belgium | Luxembourg |
|---|---|

7.   NORWEGIAN KRONE GROUP

| Denmark | Sweden | Finland |
|---|---|---|

8.   SDR GROUP

| Australia | Kuwait | Saudi Arabia |
|---|---|---|
| Bahrain | Lebanon | South Africa |
| Burma | Malawi | Tunisia |
| Cyprus | Malta | Turkey |
| Greece | Mauritius | United Arab |
| Iceland | Morocco | Emirates |
| Iran | New Zealand | Yugoslavia |
| Jordan | Nigeria | |
| Khmer | Qatar | |

# 7 Formalities and Procedural Matters

In setting up a foreign exchange dealing relationship with a bank there are normally a number of formalities to be observed which are designed to protect the two parties to the deals, that is the company and the bank, against various types of risk. These risks include unauthorised deals being done by members of the company staff, settlement risk and forward exposure risks. These risks will be analysed in turn together with procedures which may be adopted to handle them in practice.

## Authority

It is important, both from the point of view of the company and of the bank with whom it is dealing, that instructions to do deals on behalf of the company shall only be accepted by the bank as valid if they come from particular individuals nominated by the company. There is a particular problem in the foreign exchange market in that it is normal for many deals to be conducted by telephone, or telex, so that the bank does not have the customer's signature on an instruction at the time the deal is struck.

A normal banking mandate authorises the bank to carry out transactions on behalf of its customer only on receipt of the signed instruction of a duly authorised officer of the company. Most of the time no such instruction will exist in foreign exchange deals. For this reason many banks ask their customers to complete a further form of mandate for foreign exchange business which authorises the bank to accept verbal or telex instructions from named individuals as good authority to deal in the company's name. This mandate is often backed up by a Board Resolution whereby the company confirms the list of names so authorised. From the company's point of view it may be a useful safeguard, even when dealing with banks which do not operate this system, to supply the bank with a list of the names authorised to deal on the company's behalf with an instruction to the bank not to accept instructions from people other than those listed.


## Confirmations

A further safeguard for both parties is in the exchange of confirmations. Ideally the company should arrange that its banker's confirmations of foreign exchange deals should be sent to someone other than the person who has done the deal. Thus, in the event of exchange deals of an unauthorised type being carried out by a member of the treasury staff, or indeed by anyone else, the problem should come to light fairly swiftly. Clearly it will not come to light if the confirmation is sent direct to the person carrying out the unauthorised deals.

Equally, it is a point of good practice and safety if deals done on the telephone are confirmed the same day by telex. This may not help too much to protect against unauthorised dealings but it does provide a written record of what is done, which is useful in the event of any difference arising later. If this confirmation arrives the same day as the deal was done and there is a discrepancy, it will be cheaper to put matters right than if the difference is only noticed several days later, by which time one is involved in rather inconclusive arguments about who said what on the phone. Such a confirmation telex should be clearly identified as a confirmation. It must not be allowed to resemble an instruction to do a foreign exchange deal, as otherwise the company may find the bank has carried out two deals on its behalf, one on the telephone and a second following what was believed to be a telex instruction.

Here the simplest formula is the best and the telex should commence –

> 'We hereby confirm the deal done by telephone with you earlier today whereby we bought DMarks 6 million against US dollars for value 23 July 1982 at a rate of 1·8790. From John Smith, Widget Co.'

This telex confirmation should, of course, be followed up in the normal way by a mail confirmation which will include the settlement instructions for the deal. The mail confirmation should at least contain

- the name of the company;
- the date on which the deal was done;
- whether it was a purchase or a sale;
- the value date or settlement date for the deal;
- the amounts of currencies involved;
- the exchange rate agreed;
- authorised signatures.

All of these points will then be checked on receipt by the bank. In practice much more information than this is provided on the customer's mail confirmation such as

- name of individual handling any queries on behalf of the company with telephone and extension numbers;
- payment instructions, e.g. 'please remit by telegraphic transfer under advice quoting our reference number 0607745/NC, the sum of DM6,000,000, to Deutsche Industrie Bank AG, Frankfurt, account Bochum Office for credit to the a/c of Deutsche Widget GmbH, Landstrasse 17,4630 Bochum, debiting our US $ a/c with you';
- company's own reference number in event of queries;
- the name of the bank's dealer with whom the deal was agreed;
- whether the deal was done by phone or telex and if by phone whether telex confirmed separately.

Equally, the bank's confirmation to the customer should also be checked to make sure no misunderstandings have arisen. It is very rare for these aspects to create any problem in day-to-day dealings but when mistakes occur they can be very expensive.

Occasionally a company employs a new member of staff in its Treasury Department without advising its bank. Normal practice is for the bank to decline to deal with a stranger without first phoning back to one of the people known to the bank. The company is then asked to confirm the new appointment in writing.

## Risk on Unmatured Forward Contracts

When a bank contracts a forward foreign exchange deal with its customer, it will 'lay off' the deal by dealing in the market with someone else in order to finish up with a square position.

Now, suppose the bank's customer goes bankrupt before its contract matures. The bank then knows that it will not receive the funds from the customer to enable it to satisfy the matching deals done in the market. The bank will therefore have to go out and buy the necessary funds to meet these deals at the current market rate. This current rate of exchange may well be very different from that at which the deals were originally struck.

The extent of this difference will be a loss to the bank resulting from the financial failure of its customer. It might of course equally well turn out to be a profit to the bank, but credit analysts habitually tend to take the gloomiest possible view and assume that all such differences will in fact turn out to be losses.

Clearly, any bank is going to set a limit on the extent of the risk it is prepared to run on every customer on its books and this credit assessment is done in the normal manner by reference to the company's balance sheet, and other indicators of general financial strength. The setting of a limit is precisely analogous to setting a limit for amount and period for an unsecured loan. What is less easy to establish is the extent of the risk represented by an unmatured forward contract. Various banks operate different methods of assessing and controlling the risk involved. Simplest of all is to limit the total deals outstanding to each counterparty as a gross total. This implies that all unmatured deals represent a uniform degree of risk. A first improvement on this method is to accept that deals with a short original maturity involve less risk than longer ones and to allow for that in calculating exposure. Some banks having rather more sophisticated computer systems handling their exposure to each customer also allow for such things as differences in past rate volatility as between currencies or whether the existing contracts would currently show a profit or a loss if the customer failed and it was necessary to replace them at today's market rates.

## Settlement Risk

There is a second and more immediate form of counterparty risk in foreign exchange deals known as 'Settlement Risk'. This can arise if the customer fails to deliver the currency to the bank on settlement day and then goes bankrupt. Because the settlement of a foreign exchange contract is simultaneous (that is, the bank pays away the currency due to the customer or his supplier in expectation of simultaneously receiving the countervalue from the customer), the bank is usually not in a position to ensure that it has received the countervalue before irreversibly paying away the currency amount. Therefore if the customer fails at this point, the bank has lost the entire amount of money paid away. This risk is present only on the settlement day and represents either a one or a two day unsecured risk on the customer, depending on which two currencies are involved in the foreign exchange deal.

Thus most banks will operate a system of settlement limits, fixing a maximum amount for the settlement to be made on one date for each customer without prior confirmation of receipt of countervalue. There are of course a number of ways in which a bank can arrange that it has such confirmation, so avoiding any problem of this kind. For instance:

1. Settlement without any specific payment in from the customer by debit to his account at the bank, either reducing his credit balance or increasing his debit balance within an existing facility limit.

2. Requiring good settlement (see Chapter 8 for a more detailed discussion concerning 'good settlement') one day ahead of value date.

3. Waiting until the bank has received good settlement and only then issuing instructions to pay away the counter-value.

Both limits for 'unmatured forwards risk' and for 'settlement risk' are set as reasonable sized unsecured risks for the bank to take *vis-à-vis* a given customer. There will be cases where these limits set by balance sheet criteria are inadequate for the company to conduct its normal level of international business, so that the bank may seek further security either as deposited margin, or by way of guarantees from parent companies, or by way of actual physical security, as a condition of doing the business.

# 8   What is Good Settlement?

Every foreign exchange contract or international payment has a 'settlement date' or 'value date'. We now turn to the often neglected subject of what exactly constitutes 'settlement for good value' or 'good settlement' on a given date and the related subject of the time taken to effect good value for international payments. This can most conveniently be taken in four sections:
- good value for sterling;
- good value for dollars;
- good value for European currencies;
- good value for Far Eastern currencies.

## Good Value for Sterling Payments

Good settlement in the City of London is receipt before 12 noon on settlement day of a town cheque or a banker's payment. A town cheque is a cheque drawn on the *City* branch of a *clearing* bank.

Note that town cheques of less than £5,000 or cheques drawn on a non-clearer in the City, take an extra day in the clearing. Cheques drawn on non-City branches in London, or worst of all drawn on country branches, are not good settlement for several days due to delays in the clearing. Country cheques take at least three days to clear.

For the receiving bank there is an important distinction even between a town cheque and a banker's payment, as at least in theory a town cheque could bounce. A banker's payment will not normally be issued unless the customer has funds at his clearer's accounts, and is thus better even for a City based customer. If a clearing bank branch is simply asked to pay sterling to another bank by banker's payment, the payment will normally be sent by post. So the company must specifically ask for funds to be telex transferred. Then the branch will telex its City Head Office which will send round the banker's payment on the 'walks' to whichever bank is specified by the customer.

For those unfamiliar with this delightful piece of City jargon, 'the walks' are the network of bank messengers who literally walk from bank to bank within the City of London delivering all kinds of interbank messages, confirmations, advices and, above all, banker's payments. As will be apparent from the following sections, this remarkably simple arrangement provides one of the fastest settlement systems in the world.

## Good Value in European Currencies

Whereas 'same day' settlement can usually be made in US dollars or Canadian dollars this cannot normally be achieved for settlements in European currencies. Since Europe is physically close to the London market whereas New York is physically distant, this is at first sight puzzling. The reason is that New York is about half a working day behind London time, whereas Europe is up to two hours ahead of London time. If instructions are received before noon in London and processed by 3 p.m., this corresponds roughly to the opening of business in New York but is just about business closing time in, say, Helsinki.

Instructions are normally accepted two days ahead of value date, but if necessary payment 'value tomorrow' can normally be made in cities having an international money market, provided instructions are received prior to 12 noon London time. Payment in other centres is effected through the domestic clearing system of the country concerned and an additional day should be allowed.

VALUE DATES ON CHEQUES IN EUROPEAN CENTRES

Practice varies considerably not only between European countries but also as between banks in one country. Cheques deposited may become credited to the account anywhere from 'same day' to 5 days later, according to local practice. Even then, in some countries funds may not be available for outward payments until the day after clearing. Since value dating practice varies so widely, treasurers will need to find out exactly what conventions are applied by their own banks in order to avoid 'wasted' liquid funds.

Since cheques, giro credits, and other payment instruments are normally sent by mail, it is useful to have some kind of ready reckoner as to the time likely to be taken en route. As is apparent from the table below, actual mail times are surprisingly long, and have by and large continued to deteriorate in recent years. The time saving achieved by telex transfer of funds can therefore be considerable.

AVERAGE MAIL TIMES BETWEEN FINANCIAL CENTRES

|  | days |
|---|---|
| Switzerland | 1 |
| France/Belgium/W. Germany/Scandinavia/ | |
| Luxembourg/Austria/Eire | 1½ |
| UK/US/Netherlands/Spain/Canada | 2 |
| Italy | 6 |
| Add for Atlantic crossing | 2½ |
| Add for UK or Eire/continent crossing | 2½ |
| Add for UK/Eire crossing | nil |

How to use the table:

*a*: Within one country
   Use the table direct; e.g. Zurich to Geneva 1 day, Milan to Rome 6 days.

*b*: Continental Europe
   Add the figures for the country of origin and destination; e.g. Amsterdam to Paris 1½ + 1½ = 3 days

*c*: Involving sea crossings
   As *b*, but adding the 2½ days for the crossing; e.g. Frankfurt to London 1½ + 2 + 2½ = 6 days

Note that average mail times continent to UK are no faster than continent to US. These mail times are those between major cities, mail times to and from country districts may be considerably greater than those shown.

### Good Value in Japanese Yen, Australian Dollar and Other Far Eastern Currencies

These countries are effectively a full working day ahead of London. Therefore, settlement more rapid than spot value is not normally possible, even for payment to an account with a bank in Tokyo, Sydney or Hong Kong. Here again, payment in other centres will require an additional day.

**Good Value in US dollars**

(Mechanism prior to 1 October 1981.)

All Eurodollar and US dollar foreign exchange contracts are contracted for settlement at a New York bank in 'New York Clearing House Funds'. This provides good value with respect to another external payment but it is not good value for a domestic payment within the United States until the following business day. Only then are the funds actually collected from the New York clearing system and available to the local banking system. These collected proceeds are known by a bewildering variety of names including 'Cleared Funds', 'Collected Funds', 'Immediately Available Funds' or, least accurately but most commonly, 'Federal Funds'.

The distinction between 'NY Clearing House Funds' settlement and the corresponding 'Fed. Funds' settlement one day later is vital to the understanding of the US dollar settlement procedure. One of the more important results of the 'two funds' settlement is illustrated thus:

A contract providing good settlement in NY Clearing House Funds on 'day 1' will provide –

    *a*: good settlement for any foreign exchange payment or Eurodollar transaction also for settlement in NY Clearing House Funds on day 1, or

    *b*: good settlement for any domestic US payment in Fed. Funds in New York City on day 2, and also onwards to major US cities via the Fed. Wire service;

    *c*: good settlement for any domestic payment in Fed. Funds outside these cities on day 3, or later in country areas.

Naturally these differences provide a tremendous source of misunderstandings in payments between European and US firms. Europeans make US dollar payments to US firms and reasonably enough specify the value date as the date when payment is due, say, to a manufacturer in Oklahoma. The banking system always assumes that value dates on international US dollar payments are NY Clearing House Funds value dates unless the customer specifies otherwise. So in the above example the manufacturer in Oklahoma will be paid two days late whilst the European believes he has paid on time. Often this may not matter much, but sometimes it can be very important indeed. For instance, many ship charter agreements specify that late payment, even by one day, terminates the agreement and the owner has the right to reclaim the vessel and recharter. A simple misunderstanding about the clearing system can cost the charterer a considerable sum of money. It is recommended that any contract specifying payment dates for US dollars states specifically whether the payment date refers to NY Clearing House Funds or Fed. Funds available in New York City, or Fed. Funds available somewhere else specified.

In London and the principal European centres, NY Clearing House Funds payments are usually made for value spot, i.e. two days ahead. But if necessary, payment in NY Clearing House Funds can be effected for 'value today' if instructions are received prior to 12 noon London time.

(Expected revision as from 1 October 1981.)

At the time of writing (mid 1981) it is planned to alter New York Clearing House Procedures to provide same day value in Fed. Funds in New York as from 1 October 1981. Assuming that this changeover occurs on schedule, the 'two funds' distinction will disappear from this date. Timing for instructions for Clearing House Funds will not be affected.

Procedure will thus become identical with the existing clearings for Canadian dollars in Montreal and Toronto, either of which can provide same day settlement in domestic funds in their respective cities.

APPENDIX

## Rate Distortions Due to 'Two Funds' Settlement in New York

*Note*
*At the time of writing it is planned to alter NY Clearing House*
*Procedures to provide same day value in Fed. Funds as from 1*
*October 1981. If this duly occurs the rate distortions outlined in this*
*Appendix will no longer arise.*

As we have seen, NY Clearing House Funds are only good value in
Fed. Funds one business day after receipt in New York. Secondly,
for most practical purposes it may be assumed that New York
banks can only obtain interest on Fed. Funds.

These two innocuous looking statements lead to various
remarkable by-products, such as that interest rates of 6% for
Wednesday dollars, 18% for Thursday dollars and 2% for Friday
dollars are in fact exactly equivalent rates. How this can be so is
explained as follows.

We will consider in turn what happens when placing one day
fixed deposits in NY Clearing House Funds starting on a Wednesday, a Thursday and a Friday, as shown in the table following. We
assume that Federal Funds yield 6% per annum.

Monday or Tuesday starts work the same way as a Wednesday
start. Naturally, a full week of Clearing House Funds earns exactly
the same as a full week of Fed. Funds – the swings cancel out. In the
above example:

| *Yield in Clearing House Funds* | |
|---|---|
| Mon–Tues | 6% p.a. |
| Tues–Wed | 6% p.a. |
| Wed–Thurs | 6% p.a. |
| Thurs–Fri | 18% p.a. |
| Fri–Sat | 2% p.a. |
| Sat–Sun | 2% p.a. |
| Sun–Mon | 2% p.a. |
| | $\overline{42} \div 7$ gives 6% |

| | Wed | Thurs | Fri | Sat | Sun | Mon | Tues |
|---|---|---|---|---|---|---|---|

*Case 1*   Wednesday Start
NY Clearing House Funds
provides Fed. Funds

Here one day's NY Clearing House Funds provide loanable Fed. Funds for 1 day at 6%. So the NYCH Funds earn 6% per annum too.

*Case 2*   Thursday Start
NY Clearing House Funds
provides Fed. Funds

Here one day's NYCH Funds provide 3 earning days for Fed. Funds at 6% per annum since the money is available in New York over the weekend. So the NYCH Funds earn $6\% \times 3 = 18\%$ per annum for one day.

*Case 3*   Friday Start
NY Clearing House Funds
provides Fed. Funds

Here 3 days' NYCH Funds provide only one earning day for Fed. Funds at 6%. So the NYCH Funds earn $6\% \div 3 = 2\%$ per annum for three days.

These day-to-day rate distortions are directly reflected in Eurodollar rates. The effect is most noticeable in the shorter period deposits but even longer dated fixed deposits are substantially affected since the first or last day of the period may be worth 18% or 2% due to the incidence of weekends. A period with a Friday end commands a better rate than a 'neutral run' since the bank has the use of (and return on) the Fed. Funds until the following Monday.

Public Holidays in New York also produce distortions on the same lines, in that the number of days revenue from Fed. Funds 'revenue days' may differ from the number of days from which NYCH funds are committed 'calendar days'. The position may be summarised as follows:

| Revenue days, difference from calendar days | Next day a holiday? | |
| --- | --- | --- |
| | No | Yes |
| *Period starts* | | |
| Mon | – | – 1 |
| Tues | – | – 1 |
| Wed | – | – 1 |
| Thurs | – | – 3 |
| Fri | – 2 | – 3 |
| *Period ends* | | |
| Mon | – | + 1 |
| Tues | – | + 1 |
| Wed | – | + 1 |
| Thurs | – | + 3 |
| Fri | + 2 | + 3 |

*Example* 1

Thursday 15 June to Friday 30 June

> Calendar days     15
> Revenue days     $15 + 2 = 17$
>
> If the 'straight run' rate for 15 days is 6% per annum.
>
> This period would be worth $6\% \times \dfrac{17}{15} = 6 \cdot 8\%$

*Example* 2

Thursday 15 June to Monday 3 July, 4 July is a New York holiday

> Calendar days     18
> Revenue days     $18 + 0 + 1 = 19$
>
> This period would be worth $6\% \times \dfrac{19}{18} = 6 \cdot 3333\%$

*Example* 3

Friday 16 June to Monday 3 July, 4 July is a New York holiday

> Calendar days     17
> Revenue days     $17 - 2 + 1 = 16$
>
> This period would be worth $6\% \times \dfrac{16}{17} = 5 \cdot 6471\%$

The distortions go even further because, as discussed before, forward premiums are calculated from interest differentials. So forward premiums for currencies against the US dollar also move in line with the distortion in the Eurodollar rates caused by the 'two funds' clearing in New York. For instance, one well known effect is to make purchase of US dollars for value Thursday more attractive than other days of the week, so the spot dollar tends to be stronger on Tuesdays (when Thursday is spot date) and weaker on Wednesdays. This weekly cycle is known in the market as the 'technical factor'. The term is sometimes seen in press reports about the market, e.g. 'the dollar was weaker today despite some assistance from the technical factor'.

# 9 Organisation of a Bank Foreign Exchange Dealing Room

Many company treasurers, who may be in regular telephone contact with their bank to transact foreign exchange business, have never seen a major foreign exchange dealing room at work. This chapter is devoted to giving an idea of what is going on at the other end of the telephone.

## The Dealing Room

There are about one thousand internationally active dealing rooms in the world today ranging from modest operations with two or three dealers, to very substantial concerns, with perhaps up to twenty dealers, and a back-up staff of some fifty further individuals.

Within the City of London, the largest single foreign exchange dealing centre in the world, there are some 300 banks who run some kind of operation in foreign exchange, of whom some 180 will in practice deal actively to a greater or lesser extent. Of this number, perhaps some thirty or forty names handle the bulk of the turnover in London. These operations are likely to have a turnover measured in billions of dollars per week for each bank.

Whilst no two dealing rooms operate in precisely the same way, they share many common characteristics. The following describes the operation of a typical substantial foreign exchange operation in London. In the main, the description would apply equally well to an operation in Paris, Frankfurt, New York or Singapore, but in London the foreign exchange brokers play a much larger role than in other centres, so it is useful to look at their particular role in the market.

## Foreign Exchange Brokers

The broker's function is to bring together the buyers and sellers amongst the banks in the London market in return for a commission, 'brokerage', for so doing. Brokers may not deal as principals, or hold any net position in currency.

Under the terms of an agreement that lasted until 2 January 1980 between the Foreign Exchange Committee of the 'British Bankers Association' and the 'Foreign Exchange and Currency Deposit Brokers Association' (FECDBA), the London banks agreed that, when dealing for marketable amounts in the principal currencies, they would deal with one another only via the brokers. In return the brokers agreed to deal only with banks and that they would not offer a service to non-bank names.

This agreement was discontinued after 2 January 1980, enabling London banks to call one another direct, or use the brokers, as they saw fit.

Banks in London therefore deal:
- with corporate customers all over the world direct by telephone or telex;
- with other London banks either through the broking system or direct by telephone or telex;
- with banks in foreign centres direct by telephone or telex, via London brokers, or via foreign brokers.

The communication system between the banks and brokers is handled by a complex system of direct lines. Any bank foreign exchange dealer works at a tailor-made desk with a variety of equipment 'built-in' to it. Prominent amongst this will be the 'board' of brokers lines. These are compact units of 40, 60 or 100 buttons, one for each direct line. Each button has a translucent top bearing the name of the relevant broker, and each button contains a small light bulb.

This system of lights, repeated on each board, tells each dealer at a glance where calls are coming from, when they have been accepted, and which lines are engaged.

A flashing light denotes an incoming call, a steady light denotes an engaged line. There are two further buttons labelled 'ring' and 'release'. Operation is simple and very fast:

|  |  |
|---|---|
| To call out: | press broker's button |
|  | press 'ring' |
| To answer incoming call: | press broker's button |
| To terminate a call: | press 'release' |

Communication with brokers to inquire after, or propose rates for, possible deals is thus immediate. Some of the conversations are shorthand in the extreme, e.g.

Dealer:   'Paris, please'
          pause whilst appropriate man in broker's office
          picks up phone
Broker:   'Yes?'
Dealer:   'How spot now?'
Broker:   'Comes at 50'
Dealer:   'OK, bye'

This conversation, indicating that the broker has a seller of French francs at a rate of 4·3650 but no buyers at present (assuming that everyone in the market is aware of the 4·36 portion of the rate), and that the dealer acknowledges this fact but does not want to propose a deal at that price, takes seven or eight seconds. Clearly the dealer can make five or six such inquiries of different brokers within the space of one minute before committing himself to the rate he quotes to the customer and have a very good idea as to his chances of laying the deal off in the market.

There are sixteen firms of brokers in the London market and whilst any individual bank will probably not have a line to every broker, each may have several lines to particular broking houses. This is because brokers specialise by currency and often have different people looking after different currencies and possibly a separate section to handle Eurodollars.

## What the Dealer Does

Whilst the broking system is, by and large, rapid and efficient it only represents one route by which the dealer can lay off a proposed deal with a customer. Ideally he might hope to 'marry' the deal with another deal for another customer later in the day, or he can hold on to the currency he has bought for a while if he believes it will appreciate during the day, or he can lay the deal off by a direct deal with a foreign bank.

Although turnover is very large, margins are very fine and exchange rates can move substantially even within seconds. So a bank will usually seek to lay off a deal done by a second deal with another counterparty within minutes, or even within seconds, of the original deal. Most banks, even if they do run positions during the day, will square their position before the close of business and 'go home square'. Other banks too are seeking to lay off deals done with their customers and, all through the day, foreign banks as well as customers will be calling the dealing room by telephone and telex to ask for foreign exchange and deposit quotes. Brokers will also be calling, asking questions such as, 'Do you have any interest in the Euros in the 3 month period at $\frac{5}{8}$?' or 'What do you make 3 month DMark in the swap now?'

So the dealer is continuously faced with decisions which must be taken virtually immediately. When a customer is calling in by telephone asking to deal, the questions the dealer must answer include all of the following:

### Questions about the Customer

Does the bank have credit lines for this customer?

If I do the deal proposed, will the total outstanding deals exceed the credit limit set for the customer?

Is the proposed deal within settlement limits for the customer?

Is the person on the phone one of the people authorised to deal on behalf of the company?

### Questions about the Rate

Is the transaction in the direction I want or is it making matters worse? (That is, a dealer long of pesetas and having difficulty in selling them on will be less keen to buy more, and more keen to sell some and will reflect this in the rate he quotes.)

What is the market rate for the currency and date asked?

How has it been moving during the day?

What factors are likely to affect the rate later today?

What likelihood is there of matching the transaction with another deal the opposite way with another customer?

What depth of market exists in the currency at the moment and can I lay the deal off easily in the market?

Is the transaction of a size that can be laid off in the market immediately, or will it have to be kept 'on the books' until it can be aggregated with other deals and then laid off?

*Questions about his Position*
Shall I lay off the deal straight away or leave the net position 'on the books' for a while, keeping the situation under review?

The dealer needs a tremendous amount of up to the minute information to be able to take these decisions correctly in an increasingly sophisticated and competitive world. So most dealers find themselves operating in a room looking more and more like a computer centre, surrounded by flashing lights, computer terminals, telex and ticker tape machines and, of course, telephones. It is this array of communications equipment which is most likely to strike the first time visitor to a dealing room. Whilst this may be very impressive for the visitor, and even a little bewildering, the purpose is entirely functional.

## Information for the Dealer

Firstly, information comes to the dealer via the continuous exchange of information with the brokers, ranging from actual rate changes to discussion as to the significance of news items or as to the reasons thought to underlie a particular rate movement that day. A similar exchange of current rates and market sentiment occurs in conversations with foreign banks which are also taking place throughout the day.

Because exchange rates can and do respond very rapidly to news of political or economic importance, it is vital for the dealing room to know what is happening at home and abroad on an up to the minute basis. The simplest way to do this is to subscribe to one of the 'Newswire' or 'News Ticker' services such as those available from Reuters, Associated Press, or Dow Jones. These services provide continuous commentary on the news of the day, key political statements, and economic statistics (such as balance of payments forecasts, or the wholesale price index change in France) as published.

In various forms News Tickers have been in use in foreign exchange dealing rooms for most of this century. More recently however a more sophisticated system has come into use alongside the older tickers – the Reuter Monitor System*. Many dealing rooms around the world today contain a number of small TV screens (more properly, video display units or VDU's) which form part of the Reuter Monitor System.

* Other systems of this type now exist, e.g. Dow Jones' Telerate.

The system is partly a news service in that the sort of information available from News Tickers can be looked up on the VDU, but it is principally an information service about exchange rates.

A number of banks in various centres around the world (principally London, Europe and the USA) supply foreign exchange rate indications through the system's own communication network direct to a computer at Reuter's Fleet Street offices. Subscribers to the system can then obtain access to this data by keying in the appropriate code on the keyboard of their VDU. The 'page' of information specified by the code is then displayed on their VDU.

But possibly the most marked area of innovation in providing information for the dealer lies in the field of in-house computer systems, which provide data direct to the dealer's desk.

## IN-HOUSE COMPUTER SYSTEMS

Increasingly banks have turned to computer systems to provide dealers with rapid access to the information they require. Generally the move to computerisation has been in three principal areas:

- recording of deals and keeping track of the net position in each currency;
- establishing total outstandings for each counterparty versus credit limits;
- calculation of exchange rates, deposit rates and derived indicators.

Some banks have computerised all three, some have computerised none. The first two categories are probably rather apparent as to aim, but it may be wondered what the purpose of the third category is.

The requirement may be illustrated thus. The dealer knows for his currency the spot rate and the forward rates for the standard fixed periods of 1, 2, 3, 6 and 12 months against the dollar. He does not know any of the following without doing some calculations:

- spot rate v sterling;
- outright rate v dollar for 3 months 17 days;
- outright rate v sterling for 3 months 17 days;
- deposit rate for 1 month 9 days;
- level of his currency with the snake (see Appendix A);
- value of his currency v the SDR (see Appendix B).

All of these questions, and some others as well, can be derived by direct calculation from current market rates for the spot and fixed period forward exchange rates. Some banks have set up computer programs to handle this arithmetic for dealers and to improve the speed of service they can provide. So dealers will also have VDU screens at their dealing desks, where they can obtain access to these types of information.

## Customer Service Dealers and Supporting Groups

In most banks the dealers specialise by currency and one man will handle say one or two currencies only, leaving the others to be handled by colleagues. This specialisation can result in difficulty in seeing the broader picture, and the ideal interbank spot DMark specialist may not necessarily be the best man to advise a customer on say the medium term outlook for sterling.

As customers have become more sophisticated and require a better service from their dealing bank, including advice, banks have trained specialist 'customer service' dealers who solely attend to customer business and leave the interbank market to other specialist dealers.

Supporting the group of dealers are a number of other groups including:

- Position Keepers, who keep a record of the net position – long or short – in each currency throughout the day and also keep track of the level of funds in each foreign bank account abroad to avoid overdrafts. For instance, if a foreign exchange contract specifies that the bank will pay the customer from ABC Bank, New York, the position keeper will ensure that adequate funds are on the account at ABC Bank to do this.
- Financial Control, who operate the accounting process for the operation and strike profit or loss figures. The same group frequently is responsible for all the data processing services the dealers require.
- Operations Group, who handle all the paperwork resulting from the deals done, including exchange control matters, the dispatch of advices, the checking of confirmations and brokers slips, and the handling of all payments arising from the deals.

# 10 How to get Good Service from your Bank

The previous chapter tried to give some insight into the atmosphere and activity in a major dealing room. The treasurer's problem is to mobilise this complex machine to work for him to his best advantage, and now we look at some of the do's and don'ts in approaching this.

Many of the issues are exactly the same as arise when using any other professional service, including the need to think out clearly what you want to do, and to be sufficiently informed about the subject to understand the significance of advice given. It may be assumed that anyone who has read this book thus far will at least have been helped over these two fundamental hurdles so we move on to more specific issues.

### Choose the Right Bank, or Banks

As mentioned earlier, there are hundreds of banks offering a service in foreign exchange, and it may seem difficult to select one for foreign exchange transactions. Even so, it must be recognised that all of these banks have specialisms of various kinds for which they are known in the market, and these specialisms may or may not be relevant to your company's requirements. For instance, many banks are mainly interbank or 'secondary' dealers and do not handle a significant amount of customer business; others concentrate on the Eurodollar market and run little or no foreign exchange operation.

In London there are perhaps forty or fifty names offering a significant service in foreign exchange to non-bank names, and even these contain many specialists by currency. Some banks for instance will run very sizeable operations in Arab or Far Eastern currencies whilst others concentrate on say the Scandinavian currencies, or even very narrow specialisms like spot dollars only. It is worthwhile to take the trouble to seek out four or five substantial dealing banks whose specialities cover the range of the company's typical requirements and to get to know the people there.

For transactions of say $100,000 equivalent and over, it is worth asking two or three of your selected banks for simultaneous quotes and dealing with the one offering the best rate at the time. Below this size the savings arising from obtaining a better rate are likely to be minimal, and seeking to obtain a competitive quote for an amount of $10,000 is likely to be regarded as simply being a nuisance. (It also looks unprofessional since simple arithmetic will show it is not worth the effort anyway.) In seeking competitive quotes there are some points to watch:

*a*: Rates move fast, so quotes must be simultaneous if they are to reflect differences in competitiveness rather than the movement that took place between phone calls. Several telephones are required.

*b*: Do not try to 'run an auction', e.g. 'I am offered a rate of 2·41 16 by X bank, can you do better?', then going back to X bank to ask if they will outbid Y bank. Most dealers will not be interested in this and will normally quote the rate at which they are prepared to deal, expecting either a 'yes' or 'no' to a deal at that rate. If the dealer is advised at the outset that he is in 'a competitive quote situation' he can be expected to quote a fine rate anyway.

*c*: In a stable market, the only differences between the quotes of different banks active in the currency may simply reflect their own position, long or short of the currency in question. By calling more than one bank, there is a better chance of finding one who wants to deal your 'way' and who will offer a favourable price.

*d*: When dealing a large amount of several million dollars equivalent it may pay *not* to ask for competitive quotes, particularly if a forward value date or a broken date is wanted. This is because if four banks are simultaneously asked their price for $10 million of, say, French francs, each of them will immediately inquire in the market as to the prospects of laying this off. So the market reacts to a demand perceived as $40 million and the price may react substantially before any business can be done. It may be better to go to one bank known by experience to have expertise in the currency and ask them their price for the amount on the understanding that other banks will not be approached. The dealer can then price keenly, knowing that the market in which he expects to lay the deal off is unaware of the transaction and is unlikely to move against him whilst he is arranging a price.

It is not only the ability to quote a competitive rate which matters in the choice of a bank for foreign exchange. Other considerations also apply, such as:

- do transactions get settled on time and without errors?
- does the bank maintain a staff of specialists to handle customer business?
- are the staff helpful and ready to give advice, suggest alternatives, and discuss market developments?

Having established a short list of banks who give a good service in the currencies that interest you, it pays to keep the list stable. In this way you can get to know the people you are dealing with on a personal basis and develop a useful level of relationship. When things go wrong, and inevitably they will from time to time, these personal links can be very important.

## Try to Avoid Misunderstandings

Which brings us to the whole subject of errors, misunderstandings and unproductive arguments of all kinds. Nothing damages a relationship more than a dismal saga of mistakes, misunderstandings and ultimately mistrust.

The first essential is clarity, and here the main problem is to state clearly whether you want to buy or to sell. The classic formula for disaster is to say to a dealer,

'Please buy marks for me.'

This innocent form of words would be quite in order as an instruction to a stockbroker, e.g.

'Please buy 10,000 ICI for me.'

But a bank acts as principal, not as broker, and the danger here is that the dealer hears 'please buy' and assumes he is buying, and therefore that the customer is selling – the reverse of what is intended.

What the customer should say is:

'Please sell marks to me.'

This ensures that the dealer is aware that he is selling, and is not buying. Even more explicit (and the standard form of words between dealers) would be:

'How do you sell me 970,000 marks against sterling for value 18 July?'

There should be no possibility of misunderstanding a question phrased like that.

The second essential is to confirm all deals done by telephone in writing either by mail or by telex, so that if anything has gone astray it can be picked up as rapidly as possible. This is both good practice and courtesy. For instance, if you think you dealt dollars against DMarks in an amount of DM1 million, and the dealer thinks he has dealt for an amount of one million dollars, the sooner the discrepancy is found, the better.

The third essential is a matter of human nature. There cannot be any market dealer anywhere who has never done a deal 'the wrong way round', or for the wrong amount, or the wrong value date, or some other major error at some time. No one is immune. So if you make a mistake, don't be afraid to say so – the sooner it gets sorted out the better.

## Know What is Possible

There are limits to the capacity of the market both in terms of the maximum size of deal that can be handled and the maximum maturity that can be dealt.

To define these limits with any accuracy is impossible as they change all the time and special deals can often be arranged for periods, or amounts, well outside the routine operating limits of the market. But one has to start somewhere to give an idea where the limits may be reached. Bearing in mind that this is a necessarily rough and ready exercise, the table following gives an idea of what can reasonably be handled in the market without special arrangement of any kind.

## Call at an Appropriate Time of Day

We have already mentioned that the dealer always looks to lay off

| Currency | Largest spot deal handled as 'Routine' $m | Longest forward maturity regularly quoted months |
|---|---|---|
| Group 1  Sterling (v dollars)  Deutsche Mark  Swiss franc  Canadian dollar | 10–20 | 24 |
| Group 2  French franc  Dutch guilder  Japanese yen | 5–10 | 12 |
| Group 3  Belgian franc  Swedish krona  Austrian schilling  Norwegian krone  Italian lira  Danish krone | 2–5 | 12 |
| Group 4  Spanish peseta  Finnish mark  Portuguese escudo  S. African rand  Australian dollar  New Zealand dollar  Hong Kong dollar  Singapore dollar  Kuwait dinar  Saudi rial | 1–2 | 6 |
| Group 5  Exotics | 1–2 | none |

a deal done with a customer, and that he may do this either through the brokers' network or direct with a foreign bank. A London dealer will usually try both, and call a bank in the country of the currency, or in the USA, or both, as well as one or two brokers.

It follows that a customer who calls at a time of day when all these options are open to the dealer may obtain a better price relative to the interbank market price. It is important to be aware, for instance, that London can deal direct with the Arabian Gulf only until about mid-morning (and not at all on Fridays); that New York, Toronto and other Eastern cities of North America are not in contact until about 14.30 London time; that Scandinavia finishes business at about 15.30 and the Continent at 16.30.

So a dealer asked to quote for Saudi rials on Thursday afternoon may not be able to lay the deal off until the following Monday (unless he can either find a counterpart in London via the brokers, or unless he makes arrangements to deal in Jeddah on Saturday – both of which have their problems) so he will quote defensively with a wide spread. Equally, a bank dealing in Finnish marks on Friday afternoon is also likely to have to wait until Monday to lay the deal off.

So try to call the dealer when the country of the currency is open, or failing that, when the US market is open. Usually this means between 09.30 and noon, or between 14.30 and 16.30.

## Help the Dealer Help You

A dealer is involved in the market all day and everyday. He accumulates a lot of experience and will acquire a market 'feel' or sensitivity to the tone of the market. His opinion is valuable. But he is also a bank employee and his training is heavily biased towards advising customers to cover exposures, or rather, biased against recommending anyone not to cover and hence speculate. What if a customer comes back to senior management and says, 'Your bank advised me to take this risk and it went wrong?' If you want a dealer's personal opinion, he will usually happily give it, but do not ask him for the bank's advice; he will think you are trying to catch him out. Instead, make it plain that you are interested in his opinion, but will reach your own decisions. That puts the responsibility for the decisions back where it belongs, with you, the customer, but provides the dealer with a means to help.

# 11 Currency Invoicing

Thus far we have looked at the problems faced by the Corporate Treasurer in doing forward exchange deals to match the company's cash flow. This is all right as far as it goes but of course the foreign exchange deal is the end of the process which starts with a contract that the company makes with a foreign counterparty for the supply of goods or services. If this contract is made in currency that fact determines the subsequent cash flow the company experiences and the necessity to cover, or not to cover, that resultant cash flow. The decision making in the currency field should start with the consideration of which currency the contract should be in in the first place.

Companies engaged in international trade are more and more concerned with decisions about the currency in which the goods should be invoiced. Whilst trading entirely in the company's home currency has the clear advantage of simplicity, many other considerations also apply – the pros and cons have to be objectively assessed.

Exporting is, almost by definition, a market orientated business. Increasingly the currency in which the goods are to be invoiced has become an important aspect of the overall marketing package perceived by the customer.

It should not be assumed that a company invoicing in currency need inevitably run a major foreign exchange risk. Indeed various means are available to hedge the initial currency exposure arising from export sales. The decision to invoice in currency is thus less a purely financial one, but, as we shall go on to demonstrate, more a facet of marketing policy.

At its simplest the exporter may decide to invoice in currency because his prospective customers prefer it that way. This preference may be evidenced in various ways. For instance:

a: In some industries the industry leader may effectively dictate the currency basis for competing firms. If the leader prices in dollars, others may also have to do so in order to remain competitive against a background of fluctuating exchange rates.

b: In a competitive situation, the buyer may find it simpler to compare prices with competitors if quotes are given in his own currency, thus increasing the chance of securing the order. A foreign buyer invoiced in his home currency is also likely to place his order earlier, as it simplifies his decision making, and also to pay earlier after receipt of invoice.

c: For some contracts, and especially in government contracts, the currency may be formally specified as a condition of the deal.

d: Smaller organisations may well prefer to be invoiced in their home currency, even at a slight price disadvantage 'for the sake of simpler administration'.

e: An appropriate currency choice may render it easier to maintain stable price lists.

Longer term objectives may also be pursued by means of an appropriate choice of invoice currency. For instance, the currency of invoicing may be selected to enable 'invisible' price changes to be made, perhaps to protect market share for short periods in line with some longer term objective. That is, a company having a substantial market share in a country expected to have a weak market for its products in the short term, may decide to invoice in a currency expected to be similarly weak. As the currency depreciates, its customer will receive an increasing discount on the goods without the company ever publicly declaring a price reduction. Thus market share can be protected (at a cost) until business conditions improve.

Similarly, a company in a strong position may well be able to specify a very strong currency as its invoice currency, thus reaping the advantage of a continuously rising return via currency appreciation, without actually having to announce any formal price increase. Other than when pursuing this kind of deliberate policy, companies invoicing in currency usually seek to cover the resultant exchange risk. Three main methods are available to render the

company immune to swings in foreign exchange rates:
  - direct forward cover
  - option date contract cover
  - overdrafts in currencies

The most appropriate solution depends upon the nature of the company's cash flow arising from its export business. The match of assets and liabilities achieved by each of these three methods is illustrated in the diagram on page 81.

### Single Receipt on Known Date

If the cash flow consists of a series of sizeable single payments due on known future dates then the normal procedure is to take out a matching series of foreign currency forward contracts. For instance, to consider an exporter of machine tools selling in US dollars. He will be concerned to protect himself against any fall in the value of the dollar. Suppose his first receipt is $48,000, due on 8 April. He would take out a contract to sell those dollars and buy sterling for settlement on 8 April, but at an exchange rate agreed today. This then fixes the sterling value to him for his future dollar receipt and renders him indifferent to market fluctuations thereafter. Similar contracts are taken out for each of the separate payments due to him.

### Single Receipt on Uncertain Date

In many industries it is not possible to know with any degree of accuracy the actual date on which payment will be received. In such cases option date contracts come into their own. An option date contract is a foreign currency forward contract exactly as before, but with the additional flexibility that the customer has the right to call for settlement of the contract on any date within a specified option period. As before, the exchange rate is fixed at the time of the deal to ensure a known sterling countervalue for the expected dollar sales proceeds. The option period is set by the customer so as to span the likely date of payment.

### Numerous Receipts on Uncertain Dates

Borrowing the currency concerned is an alternative to taking forward cover in the foreign exchange market. This is particularly

# Currency exposure on exports.

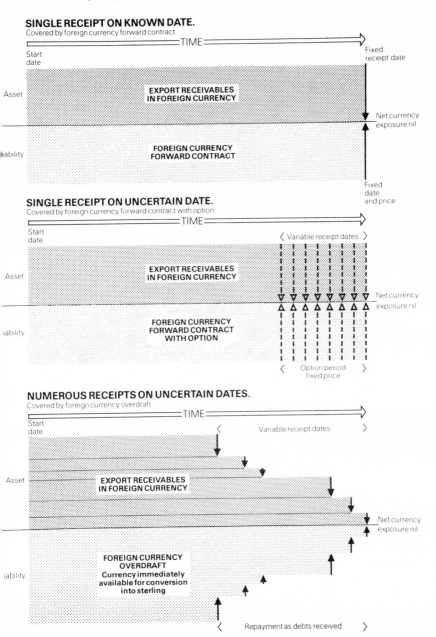

### SINGLE RECEIPT ON KNOWN DATE.
Covered by foreign currency forward contract

=====TIME=====

Start date

Fixed receipt date

Asset

**EXPORT RECEIVABLES IN FOREIGN CURRENCY**

Net currency exposure nil

Liability

**FOREIGN CURRENCY FORWARD CONTRACT**

Fixed date and price

### SINGLE RECEIPT ON UNCERTAIN DATE.
Covered by foreign currency forward contract with option

=====TIME=====

Start date

〈 Variable receipt dates 〉

Asset

**EXPORT RECEIVABLES IN FOREIGN CURRENCY**

Net currency exposure nil

Liability

**FOREIGN CURRENCY FORWARD CONTRACT WITH OPTION**

〈 Option period fixed price 〉

### NUMEROUS RECEIPTS ON UNCERTAIN DATES.
Covered by foreign currency overdraft

=====TIME=====

Start date

〈 Variable receipt dates 〉

Asset

**EXPORT RECEIVABLES IN FOREIGN CURRENCY**

Net currency exposure nil

Liability

**FOREIGN CURRENCY OVERDRAFT**
**Currency immediately available for conversion into sterling**

〈 Repayment as debts received 〉

suitable when the currency cash flow is made up from a large number of items and where payment dates are uncertain.

The principle is that the customer borrows a sufficient quantity of say, US dollars as to exactly match his receivables in US dollars. The dollars borrowed are immediately sold for sterling and the sterling used to reduce the company's sterling debt. Total borrowing is now exactly the same as before of course, but the currency make-up now differs.

As each dollar payment is received it is used in reduction of the overdraft so that the dollar receivables asset always exactly matches the dollar overdraft liability, irrespective of the amounts or dates of payments. Exchange risk is thus zero.

In practice of course such facilities operate on a rolling basis so as to keep the overall receivables book in step with the overdraft balance. The idea is often extended to increase the overdraft amount from the receivables book up to the full amount of the receivables plus the committed order book, that is, all currency assets both actual and 'in the pipeline'.

Overdraft facilities in eurocurrencies are now available in all major market currencies in the London market, although banks specialise by currency to a large extent. As in the rest of the eurocurrency market, operations in US dollars and DMarks predominate.

Suppose a UK exporter sells to the United States, Saudi Arabia, Canada, Germany, France and Sweden in local currency, and has outstandings as shown in the following table:—

| Country | Outstanding value | Exchange rate | Advance | Sterling equivalent advance |
|---|---|---|---|---|
| United States | $100,000 | 1 | 100,000 | |
| Saudi Arabia | SR788,000 | 3.32 | 237,349 | |
| Canada | C$149,000 | 1.19 | 125,210 | |
| | | | $462,559 | @  2·21 = £209,302 |
| Germany | DM100,000 | 1 | 100,000 | |
| France | FF100,000 | 2.30 | 43,478 | |
| Sweden | SwKr100,000 | 2.35 | 42,553 | |
| | | | DM186,031 | @  4·01 =  £46,392 |
| | | | | £255,694 |

Although the exporter could in theory open six separate loan accounts – one for each currency – in practice he may opt to use only two – US dollars and DMarks – to handle the income in non-European and continental European currencies respectively. This makes the two simplifying assumptions that most continental currencies are either in the 'snake' or behave as if they were, whilst most other major currencies tend to follow the dollar.

The figures quoted would allow drawings of $462,559 and DM186,031. The company would then receive the sterling counter-value of these two amounts being £255,694 by credit to its sterling account and debit to the two new loan accounts. The dollar and DMark income will go directly to reduce the loan while other currencies are first sold for dollars or DMarks and then reduce the loan.

Note that usually the company's overall borrowings will not be altered by entering into a currency overdraft; the currencies drawn will be used to pay down the company's ordinary sterling overdraft account. Total debt is not changed, it is the currency mix of the debt that is affected. Interest will be calculated day to day on the balance actually used. The method provides a means of exchange hedging combined with economical finance.

**The Rolling Overdraft**

As mentioned above, most currency overdrafts operate on a 'rolling' basis, continually adjusting to the current level of receivables by drawing down against the facility. At first sight no new complications ensue; all one has to do is to check the level of the overdraft against the receivables book from time to time and top up as required. But this approach will necessarily mean that the average level of the overdraft will always be less than the average level of receivables; only immediately after a drawing will they be identical, at all other times the overdraft level will be less than receivables. Consider for instance a company having receivables of $2,000,000 and an initial overdraft also of $2,000,000. After a few weeks the money received from customers will have reduced the overdraft down to, say $1,860,000 whereas the receivables book is still likely to be at around $2,000,000 as new sales will have been booked in the meantime. This shortfall is an exchange risk. To eliminate it procedures have to be modified a little. At least three methods are used to do this:

1. Do not use the actual receipts of currency to pay down the overdraft, but sell them spot for the home currency. Maintain the balance on the account static or nearly so, only altering it to reflect changes in the size of the receivables book.

2. Method (1) may violate the terms of the overdraft facility, which may require the receivables to be used to pay down the loan. (Self-liquidating loan principle.) In this event, agree that drawings will be made in round amounts of say $100,000 and draw down whenever the overdraft level falls to the level of receivables less *half* this amount (i.e. if receivables now $3,260,000 then draw down $100,000 as soon as overdraft balance less than $3,210,000.) This will produce a pattern where the average level of the overdraft is equal to the average receivables, varying ± $50,000 either side.

3. Method (2) may also violate the terms of some facilities which may specify that drawings may not exceed receivables at the time. In this event, the only way to cover the resultant net exposure is by forward contract. Note that if the facility is topped up to 100% of receivables every time it has dipped by $100,000, then the average exposure to be covered by forward contract (to the estimated date of next top-up) is $50,000, not $100,000.

### Currency Clauses

Sometimes an export salesman of one company and the chief buyer of another company may fail to agree about the currency to be used and they may decide to compromise on the issue by the use of a currency clause. A typical currency clause might say that the contract will be a French franc contract so drawn that the amount payable in francs will vary directly with the exchange rate between French francs and, say, sterling existing at the date of payment. It may even have been agreed that there will be some range of fluctuation that will be allowed before this clause acts so that there does not have to be continual adjustment of the rate.

At first glance this seems to solve the problem – the UK supplier of goods to France appears to have his currency risk covered – if sterling moves relative to the French franc more than so much, then he will receive an amount of francs which will be more or less enough to compensate for the movement when he sells it back into sterling. His French customer meanwhile has no involvement in foreign currency at all as he is making all his payments in francs. Unfortunately, these kinds of arrangements often result in satisfying no one for the following reasons.

The principal reason is that because there is usually some allowed fluctuation before the clause is triggered, the UK supplier will probably feel that he is always slightly behind the game and therefore losing out. More seriously, the French importer, who has an undoubted foreign/exchange risk, will not be permitted under local exchange control regulations to cover the risk by buying sterling. The authorities will argue, reasonably enough, that he has no contract to pay sterling to anybody and therefore will not be permitted to buy any. If he, in his normal course of commercial business, has signed a price clause of some kind, that is his affair and nothing to do with the exchange control authorities. By and large both parties will be better off either to invoice directly in sterling or to invoice directly in French francs by adjusting the price if necessary to reflect the cost of forward cover between the two currencies.

## Capital Projects, Special Problems

ESCALATOR CLAUSE

A more recent feature of large capital projects to be delivered over a period of years, usually to a government buyer, is that the inflation escalation clause will be geared to the inflation rate in the country of the currency of the contract and not to the inflation rate of the country of the supplier if this is different. That is to say, a French supplier of capital goods to Saudi Arabia who decided to invoice in dollars will find that the escalation clause on his contract will relate to the inflation indices in the United States, not to the rather high inflation index in France. This factor is normally more than enough to eliminate any advantage he might see in invoicing in a currency other than the French franc since the money he receives in forward premium through covering his forward contracts will be swallowed up by the difference in the inflation rate he is experiencing in producing the goods in France compared with the inflation rate he will be credited with on the contract price.

With these caveats it is more and more becoming standard practice to try to invoice in the currency of the buyer where this is a reasonably marketable currency and, where it is not, either to invoice in the currency of the supplier or the US dollar.

## Currency Tenders

There has been a longstanding problem where an exporter tenders for a contract in currency. He must give a firm price, but the exchange rate may change between the date of the tender submission date and the date the firm contract is signed. Equally the exporter is in some difficulty if he takes out forward cover to protect his position, since he may not be successful in his tender. In that event he would have to reverse his forward deal and that could be expensive. As an example, suppose a UK exporter tendering for a dollar contract to supply goods to Saudi Arabia took out forward cover for one year. In say, October, he would have sold his anticipated dollar income at an outright rate of say \$/£1·5400. So that on a million dollar contract he would be due to receive £609,756. This is fine if he gets the contract, but if six months later, in April, he learned that his tender had been unsuccessful, he would have had to unwind his deal at the new six month outright rate of say 1·4830. On the settlement date he would have to deliver £674,309 to buy back the million dollars sold in the first deal. A loss of £64,553!

Some governments in Europe and recently also the UK, have introduced insurance schemes as an alternative way to cope with this problem. The UK scheme, operated by ECGD (Exports Credits Guarantee Department) is as follows. The intending exporter agrees with ECGD the outright exchange rates on which he will base his tender. ECGD then guarantees those rates to the exporter for an agreed period of time – say three months – and receives a fee for so doing from the exporter. Supposing the exporter is successful in his tender, he covers his contract in the foreign exchange market in the usual way and ECGD take any difference, profit or loss, between this rate and the rate agreed between themselves and the exporter at the beginning.

Upon the introduction of the ECGD scheme on 1 August 1977, the arrangements were:

1. Availability – for tenders in US dollars or DMarks, other currencies by negotiation. Minimum period 3 months, maximum 9 months.

2. Cover – the exporter takes the risk himself on the first 3% of any rate fluctuation and also on any fluctuation in excess of 25%. ECGD cover the 3% to 25% range.

3. Cost – for unsuccessful tenders, a premium of £5,000 flat – for successful tenders, a premium of 3 per mille for the first 3 month period, plus 1 per mille per month for the next 3 months, plus $1\frac{1}{2}$ per mille for subsequent months up to the nine month limit. Premium payable is as above, or £5,000, whichever the greater.

   For example, for a £10 million tender out for seven months the cost would be
   – if unsuccessful £5,000
   – if successful

   | | |
   |---|---|
   | for the first 3 months | £30,000 |
   | for the next 3 months $3 \times £10,000$ per month | |
   | for the final month | $1 \times £15,000$ |
   | Total payable | £75,000 |

In the absence of these government backed insurance deals, there seems to be a continuing dilemma for the currency tender deal.


COVER FOR LONG TERM PROJECTS

Supposing a company has an export order where it agrees to supply goods invoiced in a foreign currency over a period of some five years. It can if it wishes take out forward cover for each shipment as it arises for the whole of the five year period. But for most currencies cover is only possible up to six months or one year ahead. So to begin with the exporter would perhaps only cover their first year's shipments, leaving the next four years fully exposed to exchange rate movements. There are two ways in which this uncovered exposure can be handled.

The first way is to take a five year loan in the invoiced currency, such that the loan is progressively paid back by the income from the sales of goods. The currency proceeds of the loan are immediately sold for the home currency upon receipt. Since the company then has a currency liability (the loan) and an asset in the same currency (the receivables), its exposure is hedged for the five year life of the contract. These loans can enable foreign exchange matching to be arranged over longer periods than the foreign exchange forward market normally allows. This, of course, is exactly the same principle as that discussed earlier with respect to the use of overdrafts to hedge current receivables.

The second way is consider some form of Currency Exchange Agreement (CEA): see Chapter 14.

### Equivalent Price in Foreign Currency

There is a hidden trap in setting prices in foreign currency. It is of the simplest kind, so much so that some very sophisticated treasury practitioners can fall into it every time. Suppose a company produces a product for export which it would normally sell at say £400,000, but elects for marketing reasons to price the product in Swiss francs. The Swiss franc spot exchange rate is, say Swiss francs 3·8725 equal one pound sterling. What more natural than to suppose the price should be

$$400,000 \times 3·8725 = \text{Swiss francs } 1,549,000 \text{ ?}$$

However, some pause for thought is necessary at this point. The exchange rate above is good for Swiss francs received value spot, i.e. two days hence, and for conversion to sterling then. But payment in two days is very unlikely, and it is rather more probable that payment will be received under the normal terms of the trade; say six months hence. Now, bearing in mind that had the firm initially invoiced in sterling it would have received £400,000 six months hence, what is required is the exchange rate that will similarly produce £400,000 six months hence by conversion of Swiss francs *at that time*.

It follows that the exchange rate required is the outright price for the period until payment date, here the six months outright price. (See table on page 89).

It follows that, so long as the currency price is calculated at the correct forward rate and forward contracts duly taken out, the sterling cash flow will be exactly the same irrespective of the currency in which the goods are invoiced.

For this reason it can be argued that the decision as to the invoicing currency is purely a marketing matter, with no effect upon the cash flow at all. It is tempting for the financial function to inquire why this marketing aspect is so vital, seeing that the cash

---

Equivalent Currency Price

---

1. Export price            £400,000
   Payment due in 6 months
   All costs in sterling

2. What is equivalent price for export in Swiss francs?
   Exchange Rates Swiss franc/£
         for spot delivery     3·8725
         for 6 months hence   3·6920
   We need the price which will yield £400,000 six months hence to give an
   equivalent return. That is:

   £400,000 × 3·6920 = Swiss francs 1,476,800
   not
   £400,000 × 3·8725 = Swiss francs 1,549,000 = possibly a lost order

3. Company now can:

   *a*: sell the Swiss francs 1,476,800 forward to yield £400,000 as before, or

   *b*: wait until spot and hope for better price.

---

flow is identical both ways. But the point is that although the cash flow is identical per transaction, the marketing group will no doubt assert that they will actually get more transactions done this way. The benefit arises from the improvement in the sales volume.

The whole matter may also be viewed from another angle, this time taking the position of an importer facing the prospect of taking a contract in a foreign currency. He should check that:

     *a*: there is an adequate forward exchange market in the invoice currency;

     *b*: he knows the resultant price of the goods in his home currency including the costs incurred in forward cover.

The Treasurer now finds himself with the nagging dilemma set in 3*b* of the table above. The simple thing to do would be always to cover, always guarantee the proceeds of £400,000. But will that give the best result? One structural way to at least clarify the responsibilities is to compel the marketing group to cover everything with the finance group (so that in our example they would always receive £400,000) and leave the decision as to whether or not to cover to the finance group. We now address the question of how the finance group can do this.

## Selective cover

Some companies have a policy that they do not use the forward market at all; they simply wait for the spot date and deal at the rate existing then. This is a form of inadvertent speculation as their risk is uncovered throughout. It is also poor tactics since the company must deal on the spot date however bad the market conditions happen to be on that day; there is no time left to wait until tomorrow when conditions may be more normal. Such a company's dealing is oblivious of current market conditions or the market outlook; deals are done when due.

Yet companies who always cover forward as soon as the risk is known are no better off. They too do their deals in a manner which takes no account of current market conditions or the market outlook. If they always cover three months forward, then their experience will be identical to the company that always deals spot, except that they will experience the effects of market movements three months later. Some companies, having realised this discouraging truth, have reverted to dealing spot.

Some form of selective approach is indicated, sometimes covering forward immediately, sometimes waiting before taking action. Selective cover can theoretically save money if only some satisfactory guide rules can be devised. Until more reliable forecasting techniques are available, it is always going to be something of a leap in the dark, but there are some simple risk analysis techniques that help to evaluate the sketchy data that one usually has when taking these decisions.

Suppose the company is a DMark based company and has receivables in French francs due in three months' time, and the three month discount on French francs against DMarks is 6% per annum. Cover will cost $6\% \div 4 = 1\frac{1}{2}\%$. This half of the evaluation, cost, is easy to calculate.

The other half, risk, is not. It is subjective, and quite often the most knowledgeable will be wrong. But it is necessary to obtain some measure of risk, however approximate, using all the sources of useful opinion at the company's disposal. These may be the opinions of bankers, the company's own staff in the country of the currency, professional forecasters or whatever. The objective is to obtain an estimate of the expected cost of not covering the exposure, for comparison with the known cost of cover.

The most obvious approach is to obtain direct estimates of the spot rate expected to exist in three months' time and to weight the various estimates according to the past reliability of the forecaster concerned. Suppose this estimated rate is 2½% worse than today's spot rate. This is substantially worse than would be obtained by forward cover so the company would choose to cover this particular exposure.

Slightly more sophisticated tactics have to be introduced in the case of fixed parity currencies. Looking at the above example again, but this time assuming that both currencies are members of the EMS (See Appendix A), we have to take this factor into account. Since the French franc is linked to the DMark in the EMS it is not free to just drift down. It must either devalue or stay where it is. (We are assuming a revaluation to be unlikely in our scenario.) So we have to assign a probability to whether this will happen in the three month period, assuming say that if a devaluation does occur it would be of the order of 5–7½%. One way to set out the analysis is shown below:

Q. Will French francs devalue over the next three months?

| Source of opinion | 1 Weight given to opinion | 2 Probability assigned % | 3 $1 \times 2$ |
|---|---|---|---|
| Bank X | 1 | 20 | 20 |
| Bank Y | $\frac{3}{4}$ | 10 | 7·5 |
| Forecasting Co | $1\frac{1}{4}$ | 30 | 37·5 |
| French Co | 2 | 40 | 80 |
| Internal economist | 1 | 40 | 40 |
| Totals | 6 | | 185·0 |

So we have the weighted opinion (total column 3 divided by total column 1) that there is a 31% likelihood of a 5–7½% devaluation.

So expected cost of 'no cover' is

$$\frac{31}{100} \times \frac{5 + 7\frac{1}{2}\%}{2} = 1\cdot94\%$$

Of course this is a very primitive type of calculation; many more sophisticated calculation models are now in use, assigning differing probabilities to different ranges of outcome. That is, not only to take into account the chances of a 5–7½% devaluation, but also movements of other sizes. These more general versions of the calculation also apply to floating currencies.

A basic difficulty with these methods arises immediately. How does one obtain opinions in statistical form from the company's advisers? It clearly is not going to be possible to ask most economists what the likelihood of a ten percent improvement in sterling relative to Canadian dollars and obtain as an answer '30 per cent'. Most answers are likely to be of the form 'I don't know, but it seems to me etc . . .'. The treasurer needs some device, however crude, to enable him to grade opinion.

A suggested scale follows. With even very slight practice, it will be found possible to grade any opinion which actually exists to the nearest ten points on the scale. Try it on yourself. Will my team win on Saturday? Obviously one cannot *know*, but the likelihood? 30? 40? Let's say 40. If we're ten points out it doesn't really matter anyway.

---

### AN OPINION SCALE

'In my opinion it is . . .

| % | | % |
|---|---|---|
| 0 | impossible | 0 |
| 10 | almost impossible | 10 |
| 20 | very unlikely | 20 |
| 30 | unlikely | 30 |
| 40 | on balance, not very likely | 40 |
| 50 | an evens bet | 50 |
| 60 | on balance, more likely than not | 60 |
| 70 | likely | 70 |
| 80 | very likely | 80 |
| 90 | almost certain | 90 |
| 100 | certain | 100 |

. . . that this will happen'

---

### RISK AVERSION AND DECISION RULES

The above two decisions were both rather obvious. They may be illustrated thus:

| Case | 1<br>Known cost<br>of full<br>cover % | 2<br>Estimated<br>cost of<br>'No cover' % | 3<br>= 1 ÷ 2<br>cost<br>ratio | Decision |
|------|------|------|------|------|
| 3 month FF Case 1 | 1·5 | 2·5 | 0·6 | Cover |
| 3 month FF Case 2 | 1·5 | 1·94 | 0·77 | Cover |

In both cases it was seen likely to be cheaper to cover than not to, and so cover would be taken. But what if column 2 had come out at 1·4%? Would it be so obvious that the decision should be not to cover? Companies must decide their degree of risk aversion here. A convenient way for the treasury function to do this is to make the size of the ratio in column 3 an automatic determinant of action. For instance, the decision rules might be:

> If ratio is 0 to 0·9      cover
> If ratio is 0·9 to 1·2    refer
> If ratio is 1·2 plus      do not cover

The company's degree of risk aversion can be set by agreeing the numbers to be used in the above three rules.

The advantage of this approach is that the Board is able to specify to the Treasurer that he is to take his decisions according to the set criteria, is to follow a standard calculation procedure in arriving at the cost ratios and is to keep adequate records of the input data to the calculations and the transactions done. This enables the Board to set policy on an overall rather than a 'per occasion' basis, yet gives the Treasurer rather specific directives with authority to act within them. This is a valuable aid to clarifying responsibilities whilst enabling Treasurers to act immediately in the market place as appropriate.

The Treasurer still appears to be left in an unresolved quandary when this routine shows up the result 'refer'. Fortunately even this situation can be reasonably adequately resolved. Firstly, the very fact of being in this situation means that the relative costs of 'cover' and 'no cover' are expected to be very similar. So it may not matter too much which course is adopted. Secondly, since all the more obvious decisions are already clearly indicated by the routine, attention can be directed to further analysis of the pros and cons of covering the more borderline cases. Further, the issue is not quite as black and white as the foregoing argument may have made it appear. There is always the possibility to cover for a part of the amount only, wait for a week or so, and then look at the problem again.

The important thing is to record how the decision taken was arrived at and what considerations were felt to be important at the time. We all learn from our mistakes, and have more opportunity to do so if the reasons for the original decisions are recorded and can be referred back to.

Mistakes include getting it right by accident. This is only achievable by getting at least two things wrong at the same time, which happen to have cancelled out. It is vital that the records show this, so that false confidence is not built up, leading to less happy repetition of one of the previous mistakes.

Many companies have found that the steadily accumulating body of documented experience provides one of the more valuable end products of this kind of highly structured approach.

### SPECULATION

There may seem to be a thin and uncertain line between 'selective cover' and 'speculation'. Apart from the fact that in many European countries true speculation would be impossible under local Exchange Control regulations, speculation is rare among commercial firms.

Most people would accept that if they have an exposure arising in their normal trading business of $X one month forward, then decisions about whether or not to take forward cover of $X are 'selective cover' and a normal prudent business practice. Most people would also accept that to deal for $10X instead of $X because the treasury felt they could make a profit on the foreign exchange would be speculation.

On these definitions 'selective cover' is a defensively motivated attempt to contain costs; 'speculation' is seeking to turn profit on deals that have no relation to any underlying commercial transaction arising from the company's normal business.

# 12 'Balance Sheet' or 'Translation' Exposure

The impact upon a company of foreign exchange movements arises in two ways. The first, which we have considered so far, arises from transactions done and committed in foreign currencies. The other arises from the translation of the currency balance sheets of foreign subsidiaries. These two types of risk are usually referred to as 'cash flow risk' and 'balance sheet risk', or sometimes as 'transaction risk' and 'translation risk'.

At its simplest the parent company is exposed in the currency of the subsidiary to the entire net worth of the subsidiary (assuming that all the items in the subsidiary's balance sheets are in its local currency). As soon as a company sets up a foreign subsidiary it creates a translation risk. But the existence of this risk is rarely a consideration in the decision as to whether or not to set the subsidiary up, which most of the time is quite rightly decided on long run commercial and political considerations. Thereafter the company is not usually at liberty to decide, at least in the short run, to reverse their decision and take the factory home. Once it is there, it is there – and the exposure is there as well.

One of the resultant dilemmas may be illustrated thus. A company may be a major exporter to a third world country which, although a big market, has a weak currency. For competitive reasons it is necessary to invoice everything in the local weak currency. This situation creates very heavy cash flow exposure. The company may therefore decide to set up a production facility in that country in an attempt to match the cash flow exposure a little better. Normally it will succeed in reducing cash flow exposure by doing this, but will create a new balance sheet exposure. The exposure is of known size but unknown duration.

In fact, as we shall see, there is room for some debate as to how the size of the exposure should be calculated and in particular whether this figure can be directly derived from financial accounts. The first problem is that there are several alternative conventions in use for the preparation of financial accounts, and this we turn to next.

## Accounting Exposure

All companies having foreign subsidiaries are obliged to translate their subsidiaries' balance sheets into the parent company's currency for the purpose of consolidation. There are really only two possible rates of exchange that can be used to translate any particular asset or liability:

> $a$: the exchange rate ruling at the balance sheet date, or 'closing rate', or
>
> $b$: the exchange rate ruling at the transaction date, or 'historical rate'.

Various accounting models have been used in the past, based upon different combinations of the use of closing rates and historical rates for different classes of assets. Over time, these many variations have been gradually whittled down to just two principal methods: these are the 'closing rate method' and the 'temporal method'.

### THE CLOSING RATE METHOD

All items in balance sheets of subsidiary companies are translated at exchange rates ruling on the balance sheet date. As exchange rates change the parent company will experience a gain or loss relative to the previous balance sheet date as the subsidiary's net worth changes in terms of the parent company's currency. These gains or losses are treated as capital items in the consolidated accounts, being handled as movements in capital reserves.

Gains or losses made by the subsidiary company from currency transactions entered into as part of its trading operations form part of its own profit and loss account. The P & L account may be translated at either the closing rate or at an average rate for the accounting period for purposes of consolidation.

Similarly, gains or losses made by the parent company from currency transactions entered into as part of its trading operations go direct to P & L account. Exceptions are made in the case of loans or forward contracts made in order to hedge the currency exposure represented by the net worth of the subsidiary (usually in rather tightly defined circumstances) and in such cases gains or losses are taken to capital reserve as offsets to the movement due to change in net worth.

## The Case for the Closing Rate Method

The closing rate method is based on what is known as the 'net investment concept'. That is, the parent is considered to have a net investment in its foreign subsidiary and that the whole net worth of that subsidiary is at risk from currency fluctuation. The implication is that the subsidiary is substantially an independently operating business, perhaps locally financed.

The method seems the natural choice where this is the case; fixed assets financed by local borrowings will net off under the closing rate method which seems the natural result, but would not do so under the temporal method – historic cost of the asset would be fixed in terms of the parent's currency but the size of the borrowing would fluctuate with the exchange rate.

This advantage also illustrates a major difficulty of principle. In the case of currency appreciation, the closing rate method will 'upvalue' the fixed asset in the books of the parent, so bringing a gain into account prior to disposal of the asset, contrary to normal accounting principles. However, proponents of the closing rate approach dispute that this is a valid objection.

Firstly, they argue that the historical cost of an asset acquired by a foreign corporation can be measured only in the foreign currency concerned and that the asset has no historical cost in the currency of the parent. Translating that cost at current rate does not on this view represent a departure from the historical cost principle – the foreign currency cost is the only historical cost.

Secondly, it may be reasonably validly stated that particular assets and liabilities for a subsidiary operation are not individually at risk, rather the whole enterprise is at risk. Only by translating the whole balance sheet at current rate can economic risk be approximated.

A less contentious argument in favour of the closing rate method is that the method accurately translates the subsidiary's existing balance sheet ratios. This is not the case where historical rates are used for translating certain assets.

## THE TEMPORAL.METHOD

The temporal method distinguishes between those items recorded in the balance sheet at historical cost, and those recorded at current values. Items showing at historical cost are translated at the rate of exchange ruling at the time the item arose (hence 'temporal') whereas items shown at current value are translated at the current market rate, or 'closing rate', as above. The difference between the two methods is shown in the table below:

| Method | Temporal | Closing Rate |
|---|---|---|
| *Assets* | | |
| Cash | * | * |
| Securities at cost | H | * |
| Securities at market | * | * |
| Receivables | * | * |
| Inventory | | |
|   at replacement | * | * |
|   at cost | H | * |
|   at market | * | * |
| Property plant and equipment | H | * |
| Depreciation | H | * |
| Goodwill | H | * |
| Intangibles | H | * |
| *Liabilities* | | |
| Overdrafts, etc | * | * |
| Payables | * | * |
| Long term debt | * | * |

\* Translate at current rate.

H Translate at historical rate (i.e. the exchange rate existing at the time the asset was originally acquired).

Under the temporal method exchange differences arise upon consolidation owing to the fact that part of the balance sheet varies with current exchange rates whilst part does not. Such exchange differences are taken direct to the consolidated P & L account, and are not treated as movements in reserve accounts.

### The Case for the Temporal Method
The concept underlying the temporal method is that the foreign operations are a simple extension of the activities of the parent. The method seeks to develop consolidated accounts that would not differ appreciably from those that would have resulted had all

the group's operations been domestic. It follows that, under this reasoning, historical cost items should have a value fixed in the currency of the parent, whereas items valued at current valuation carry the 'current valuation' idea through to the exchange rate as well.

The method avoids the accounting principle difficulty arising with the closing rate method which, as argued above, can imply that gains could be taken into profit and loss account on assets valued at cost prior to disposal.

The major defect of the temporal method arises where it is used to consolidate the accounts of a typical self-contained subsidiary company. Usually it will give a negative 'exposed net worth' which is contrary to commonsense criteria.

The question is illustrated in the table below. Clearly, items valued at historical cost are not exposed to currency movements, although those valued at current rates are.

The example shows a small subsidiary with an accounting exposure under the temporal method of £25,000, net liability. That is, if sterling rises 10% the consolidated P & L account will show a *loss* of £2,500.

| | £ | Accounting exposure | |
| | | Temporal | Closing Rate |
|---|---|---|---|
| *Assets* | | | |
| Cash | 20,000 | 20,000 | 20,000 |
| Receivables | 15,000 | 15,000 | 15,000 |
| Land | 60,000 | – | 60,000 |
| *Liabilities* | | | |
| Payables | 25,000 | 25,000 | 25,000 |
| Local debt | 35,000 | 35,000 | 35,000 |
| Capital funds | 35,000 | | |
| | 95,000 | | |
| Net Exposed Assets | | (25,000) | 35,000 |

Proponents of the temporal method admit that the closing rate method would be more likely to lead to a measure of exposure more compatible with economic exposure, but point out that the normal limitations of financial accounts still would not permit direct calculation of economic exposure.

Why it would not may be simply illustrated. Consider the subsidiary balance sheet shown above.

Both methods agree that, other than the Land item (the only item in this balance sheet at historical cost), the accounting exposure is a net liability of £25,000. The temporal method translates land as a fixed asset at historical cost so that it is not considered as an accounting exposure. However, the closing rate method treats all assets as exposed, thus according to that method overall accounting exposure is equal to overall net assets:

$$£60,000 - £25,000 = £35,000 \text{ net asset}$$

The economic exposure relates to the current value of the land at the current market rate. Now the price of land may well not have moved in line with exchange rates – it is after all an entirely unrelated market – and the value of the land may now be say £116,000. Economic exposure is thus:

$$£116,000 - £25,000 = £91,000 \text{ net asset}$$

So whilst the closing rate method gives a result closer to economic exposure than the temporal method (which here even shows an accounting exposure as a net liability whilst economic exposure is a net asset) it still does not calculate economic exposure direct.

### Translation Standards in the USA

The first accounting standard in this area was produced by the Financial Accounting Standards Board in October 1975. Their Financial Accounting Standard No. 8, hereafter 'FAS 8' was a massive document running to over a hundred pages, mainly taken up with detailed arguments for and against various translation methods. The outcome was a straight adoption of the temporal method with all resultant exchange differences taken direct to P & L account. Use of equalisation accounts, reserves, and other smoothing techniques was disallowed.

The standard attracted widespread criticism in practice, owing to the wild (and often logically perverse) swings in reported consolidated earnings. A major reappraisal of the whole subject was then instigated resulting in the publication of a 'Proposed Statement of Financial Accounting Standards' on 28 August 1980.

The best summary of this document is probably their own, and it is therefore directly quoted below:

SUMMARY

This proposed Statement would replace FASB Statement No. 8, Accounting for the Translation of Foreign Currency Transactions and Foreign Currency Financial Statements, and revise the existing accounting and reporting requirements for translation of foreign currency transactions and foreign currency financial statements. It proposes standards for foreign currency translation that are designed to (1) preserve the financial results and relationships as measured in the primary currency in which a foreign entity conducts its business (referred to as its 'functional currency') and (2) reflect changes in exchange rates in a manner consistent with expectations of the financial effects of those changes on the functional currency earnings generated by the foreign entity.

The basic measurement of all the elements of a foreign entity's financial statements (i.e. assets, liabilities, revenues, expenses, gains and losses) would be made in conformity with US generally accepted accounting principles in terms of its functional currency. All of a foreign entity's assets and liabilities would be translated from that functional currency into the reporting currency using the current exchange rate.

All revenues, expenses, gains, and losses would be translated to approximate the effect of using the exchange rates on the dates they are recognised.

Certain adjustments are an inherent result of the process of translating foreign entities' financial statements at exchange rates that differ from the exchange rates previously used for translation. Such translation adjustments would not be included in determining net income for the period but would be disclosed and accumulated in a separate component of consolidated stockholders' equity until substantial or complete liquidation occurs, or until permanent impairment of the related net investment in the foreign entity is determined.

An entity may engage in transactions involving currencies other than its functional currency (for example, a US company may borrow Swiss francs or a French subsidiary may have a receivable denominated in kroner from a Danish customer). Exchange gains and losses on those foreign currency transactions would generally be included in determining net income for the period in which exchange rates change.

It is seen that it represents a total change of direction from FAS 8 in that it recommends adoption of the closing rate method. The dilemma concerning the taking into account of unrealised gains on fixed assets is neatly resolved by the concept of the 'functional currency', and the preservation of conventional accounting principles in terms of the functional currency.

As stated in the summary, in the ordinary way gains and losses on foreign currency transactions are included as part of the profit and loss account. However, there are two exceptions in the detailed provisions:

    *a*: Forward contracts designed to hedge an existing currency commitment are treated as matched.

    *b*: Gains and losses arising from currency transactions designed to hedge a net investment in a foreign subsidiary, e.g. a currency loan to finance a subsidiary in Belgium are treated as matched.

The Proposed Statement is issued by the FASB for public comment, following which a possibly slightly modified version will become mandatory probably from December 1981 onwards.

### Translation Standards in the UK

On the European side of the Atlantic, most companies (around 80% in the UK according to a 1976 survey) traditionally used the closing rate method, although no accounting standard made this mandatory. This fact was naturally taken into account when compiling the first UK recommendations, Accounting Standards Committee Exposure Draft 21, published in September 1977 and hereafter called 'ED 21'. ED 21 outlined a flexible approach which allowed companies a free choice between either the temporal method or the closing rate method as the company felt was most appropriate to their needs. No other methods were recognised as acceptable.

During 1980 the UK Accounting Standards Committee (and their equivalents from Canada) were represented at the US discussions which led to the publication of the US 'Proposed Standard'. The intention was to enable all these countries to produce standards which were as closely indentical as possible. In due course therefore, the publication of a new UK Exposure Draft, 'ED 27 Accounting for Foreign Operations' was published by the ASC in October 1980.

ED 27 is, as perhaps might be expected, pitched somewhere between the earlier ED 21 and the US proposed standard. ED 27 states that the closing rate method 'should normally be used'. The usual provisions with this method are spelt out, such as that translation differences shall be taken to reserves and so on.

As implied above, a major difference is that ED 27 retains an ability to use the temporal method 'where the directors consider that it will more fairly reflect the manner in which the business is conducted'. The preamble points out that

1. 'The temporal method is based on the concept that the business of a foreign subsidiary is an extension of the holding company's own activities' and

2. 'In the UK and Ireland foreign operations are normally carried out through foreign businesses and therefore the temporal method will not normally be appropriate for use.'

Nevertheless it is not only permitted but actually required that

'In those circumstances where the trade of the subsidiary is a direct extension of the trade of the holding company the temporal method should be used.'

Treatment of the revenue of subsidiary companies is now made more specific in that the profit and loss account is required to be translated at an average rate for the period. The difference between the profit and loss account translated at an average rate and at the closing rate is to be recorded as a movement on reserves.

Arrangements analogous to those described in the case of the USA apply to the treatment of currency loans intended to hedge investment in subsidiaries.

The specific circumstances when offset is allowable are:

'(a) the exchange difference arising on loans denominated in a particular currency in any accounting period may be offset only to the extent of the exchange difference arising on foreign equity investments in the same currency;

(*b*) the relationship between the holding company and the subsidiary or associated company justifies the use of the closing rate method;

(*c*) the accounting treatment is applied consistently from period to period.' (Para. 57)

This is a little more tightly drawn than the US equivalent. However, ED 27 also provides that:

> 'An equity investment in a foreign subsidiary will normally be made by means of the purchase of shares in that subsidiary. However, long term loans between the holding company and the subsidiary and intercompany balances arising from trading operations which it is not intended should be settled currently, may be means of financing the subsidiary. In these circumstances such loans and inter-company balances should be treated as part of the holding company's equity investment in the subsidiary.' (Para. 34)

It is this area of ED 27 which has perhaps caused most criticism from Treasurers, being considered far too restrictive. Specifically it does not cover

- hedges other than by the parent company – e.g. by a fellow subsidiary;
- hedges by foreign exchange contract or futures market contracts rather than by loan;
- hedges in a parallel currency where perhaps the actual currency of exposure has no market.

A Working Party of the London 'Association of Corporate Treasurers' has suggested the following alternative wording to replace Para. 57:

'57

(*a*) Where the proceeds of foreign currency loans raised by a parent or fellow subsidiary company have been used to finance equity investments in foreign subsidiaries or associated companies or any other foreign currency denominated asset, or are effective as a hedge against such investment, differences on re-translation of the loans may be offset by differences arising on the re-translation of the related opening net assets or asset.

(b) Where forward or future foreign exchange contracts have been taken out by a parent or fellow subsidiary company with the intention of providing a currency hedge against equity investment in foreign subsidiary or associated companies or any other foreign currency denominated asset or liability, then such assets or liabilities should be re-translated at the rate of exchange effective in, and to the extent that they are covered by, such related or matching forward or future foreign exchange contracts.'

## Inflation Accounting Standards

Pioneered in the Netherlands before the Second World War, accounting for inflation has recently become a subject for draft Accounting Standards in several European countries. In the UK, a formal Accounting Standard, SSAP 16, was finally published in March 1980. The method chosen, termed Current Cost Accounting (CCA), adjusts reported revenue to cover the impact of inflation upon depreciation provisions, inventory, and monetary items of net working capital. Many further detailed provisions exist. SSAP 16 is now mandatory in the UK and Eire for all listed and large unquoted companies.

Unfortunately, all this effort seems to be unco-ordinated with that directed to Foreign Exchange Exposure; it seems that an opportunity has been missed. Both 'Accounting Exposure' and 'Inflation Adjustments' can be viewed as simply different aspects of the general problem of accounting in an environment where the value of money is subject to continuous change. Perhaps here is a useful field of endeavour for the Accounting Standards Boards; to produce a general integrated system.

## Economic Exposure

When considering the example of the Balance Sheet of a simple subsidiary during the above discussion about translation methods it was seen that the economic exposure related to the land at its market value rather than the historical cost showing in the formal accounts. The arguments mirror discussions as to why the sale value of a company is not the same as the net worth shown on the balance sheet. To calculate economic exposure, the accountant has to try to assess the market value of the assets making up the net worth. It is the net worth of the company at valuation that is exposed.

Or is it? It can be argued that only part of the net worth at valuation is exposed, as certain classes of physical asset should be excluded.

Inventory is a case in point. For a company selling similar or identical products in different countries, the inventory value to the group is not affected by a devaluation of the currency of the country where it is currently held. It can always be moved out again. Put another way, the price of the inventory at valuation should automatically rise in local currency terms to counteract the devaluation of the local currency so as to keep the value constant in external terms. Certain items of transferable plant and machinery can be regarded in the same light, 'fixed' assets or not.

Some Treasurers take this idea further, essentially arguing that even fixed assets are unaffected by local devaluations in the long run, since exchange rates eventually follow inflation. That is, if inflation in the country concerned is 10% higher than elsewhere, valuations in local currency will rise 10% per annum, but local currency will fall 10% to compensate. Elegant though this proposition may seem, it does not work other than in a general sense over a number of years as an average over a number of currencies. For most of us, this is simply not good enough; some currencies are heavily influenced by factors other than inflation, as for example, sterling in the years 1977–81. As will be seen in Chapter 15, even those showing good long run correlations can and do move 'countertrend' for periods of years.

These debates to refine the definition of 'true economic exposure' will no doubt continue, but for the moment it seems that a reasonable workable compromise is to take it to be 'net worth at valuation less transferable physical assets'. Too cumbersome a label for discussion purposes; perhaps it could be called 'Local Net Assets'?

## Tax Considerations

In most countries gains and losses arising from foreign exchange contracts placed in connection with trade or other current transactions are treated as ordinary trading income for tax purposes. Foreign exchange gains and losses of this type are thus treated in the same way as current interest; cover or interest arbitrage transactions taken within one company designed to be neutral pretax will thus also be neutral after tax.

However, in many countries this tax symmetry falls down in respect of capital items. A contract taken out to hedge exposure on a pretax basis will fail to produce a neutral result after tax because capital gains/losses may either be subject to lower rate capital taxes or not be allowable at all against either capital or income taxes. Naturally, in a notoriously complex area such as tax it is not possible to produce a complete or universally applicable set of rules as to tax treatment of currency matters without inordinate length and complication. However, to illustrate the asymmetries introduced by tax effects, we will briefly consider the position in the UK. Many other Western industrial countries operate in a broadly similar manner, although the UK treatment of currency loans appears to be a local anomaly.

### UK TAX TREATMENT OF CURRENCY ITEMS

|  | On Trading Account | On Capital Account |
|---|---|---|
| Currency Deposits |  |  |
|   FX Gain/loss | Revenue | Revenue [1] |
|   Interest receivable | Revenue | Revenue |
| Currency Loans |  |  |
|   FX Gain/loss | Revenue | Nil [2] |
|   Interest payable | Revenue | Revenue |
| Forward Contracts |  |  |
|   Unrealised Gain/loss | Revenue | Nil |
|   Realised Gain/loss | Revenue | Revenue [3] |
| Translation Gain/loss | Not applicable | Nil |

Notes:

[1] Situation may differ for investment companies, where in certain circumstances gain/loss may be treated as chargeable to capital gains tax or even as non-taxable.

[2] Treated as revenue or capital in many other countries.

[3] May be treated as capital in some countries provided that the contract is sold prior to maturity. That is, the contract itself is treated as a capital asset.

Various consequences of this pattern are of interest to the Treasurer:

> *a*: At least in the UK, a currency long term loan to finance an investment in the same currency, which logically would seem to provide a perfect economic hedge, will not hedge after tax. If the currency rises relative to sterling, then the

'gain' arising in sterling terms on the asset side will be taxable, whereas the loss arising on the loan will not be tax allowable.

Items on trading account, such as currency overdrafts against currency receivables, are all treated as revenue items subject to Corporation Tax and do enable perfect hedging both before and after tax.

*b*: Transaction exposure hedged against translation exposure pretax will not be hedged after tax. For example Widget Inc. USA has a subsidiary, Widget SA, in France. Widget Inc. has an exposure – long of French francs as a translation risk, and seeks to hedge this by running a short position of the same amount in French francs in Widget Inc., either by utilising existing French francs payables in respect of imports into the USA from France, or by direct short term borrowing. Supposing the hedge is done on a pretax basis, for an amount of FF5,000,000 when the exchange rate is $1 = FF4.00.

|  | FF | $ equiv. |
|---|---|---|
| Net exposed assets in France | 5,000,000 | 1,250,000 |
| FF borrowings in USA | (5,000,000) | (1,250,000) |
| Net | — | — |

Now assume that the French franc falls to $1 = FF5.00 and assume a US tax rate of 48%.

|  | FF | $ equiv. |
|---|---|---|
| Net exposed assets in France | 5,000,000 | 1,000,000 |
| FF borrowings in USA | (5,000,000) | (1,000,000) |
| Translation loss |  | (250,000) |
| Gain on FF borrowings |  | 250,000 |
| Tax on this gain @ 48% |  | (120,000) |
| Net Loss |  | (120,000) |

It is apparent that to achieve a true after tax hedge, the amount to be borrowed has to be grossed up to allow for the tax asymmetry if a neutral position post tax is required. The factor to be applied is:

$$\frac{1}{(1 - \text{marginal tax rate})}, \text{ here} = \frac{1}{(1 - .48)} = 1.92308$$

This means that the necessary level of French franc borrowings to hedge the original FF5,000,000 exposure is:

FF5,000,000 × 1·92308

= FF9,615,400

With this grossed up hedge the economics become:

| | FF | $ equiv |
|---|---|---|
| *Initial Position* $1 = FF4·00 | | |
| Net exposed assets in France | 5,000,000 | 1,250,000 |
| FF borrowings in USA | 9,615,400 | 2,403,850 |
| *Final Position* $1 = FF5·00 | | |
| Net exposed assets in France | 5,000,000 | 1,000,000 |
| FF borrowings in USA | 9,615,400 | 1,923,080 |
| Translation loss | | (250,000) |
| Gain on FF borrowings | | 480,770 |
| Tax on this gain @ 48% | | (230,770) |
| Net Loss | | nil |

*c*: Forward contracts taken out to hedge translation exposure pretax will not be hedged after tax. The amount of the forward contract necessary to achieve a post tax hedge has to be grossed up following the same reasoning to that outlined above under (*b*). FASB 20, issued in December 1977 as an amendment to FASB 8 contains provisions (Para. 13) to allow for grossed up hedge deals designed to net after tax to be so treated in calculating reported accounting exposure.

## Hedging Translation Exposure

There are really only three options available in handling translation exposure:

- ignore it;
- hedge it with forward contracts;
- reduce it by direct matching.

Many corporations choose to deliberately ignore the matter as a policy and direct all their currency systems to the management of cash flow exposure. This policy is not as naïve as it may at first seem; it may be seen as an assumption that, over the life of the company's fixed assets inflation differentials will in fact be compensated by equivalent exchange rate movements, coupled with a willingness to accept some volatility in reported earnings due to valuation changes from period to period.

Other corporations favour a selective use of forward foreign exchange contracts to hedge translation exposure either to reduce volatility of reported earnings or to hedge what they have identified as genuine economic translation exposure. To use the same scenario as before, Widget Inc. could hedge its translation exposure of French francs 5,000,000 by selling French francs forward in the grossed up amount of FF9,615,400. Economics are identical to those illustrated above, merely substituting 'FF forward contract' for 'FF borrowing in USA'.

The hedge has been achieved, but, as many Treasurers have learnt to their cost, the cure can be worse than the original disease. Whereas exposure is now matched, cash flow is certainly substantially distorted to achieve this. The translation gain/loss is unrealised (and in practice unrealisable in the short run), but the compensating gain/loss on the hedging forward contract is a real alteration to the company's cash position, for better or worse as the case may be. The swing in the cash position, especially of course when real cash losses are to be paid away without any available cash forthcoming from the 'compensating' unrealised translation gain, may be unacceptable from the cash management point of view. Normally hedging translation exposure will result in cash management consequences and the policy dilemmas in this area either lead to some form of muddy compromise or a decision to rely more upon direct matching to reduce translation exposure.

## Reducing Translation Exposure

Unfortunately, since accounting exposure is largely unrelated to economic exposure, deals done to cover accounting exposures may make the real position worse. So, taken together with the thorny complications due to tax and cash flow, the initial temptation to hedge accounting exposure by forward foreign exchange deals has largely faded out. In any case, usually it will not pay to hedge even economic translation exposure on a routine basis and many major multinationals do not attempt to do so. But if a company has a major exposure in a currency felt to be particularly at risk at a given time, then it will be prudent to take out forward cover on that one occasion.

More attention has been devoted to reduction of translation exposure, both economic and accounting, by direct changes to the balance sheet. Efforts to reduce exposure are usually confined to the following:

1. Making maximum use of local borrowings to finance the local subsidiary and avoiding loans from the parent company. Here it is important to ensure that local management do not succeed in getting undue emphasis placed on the high interest cost of borrowing local currency (in some countries this may be quite high) because of their lower awareness of the exchange risks involved.

2. Altering net worth by paying in extra capital or by gradual shifts in dividend policy.

3. Leading and lagging payments so as to change the net currency exposure on payables and receivables in the company's favour.

4. For a subsidiary in a weak currency area, invoicing some export sales in hard currency to counteract the basic exposure.

5. Special factors apply in some Latin American countries such as Brazil or Argentina where the currency may be devalued each month in line with inflation. Here the economic exposure on fixed assets may be genuinely zero as their dollar value may tend to remain constant. Further, some government bonds are indexed to the dollar or are 'inflation indexed'. The local subsidiary can hedge by borrowing locally to buy these indexed bonds.

**Indirect Economic Exposure**

In an international group of companies some exposures may not be what they seem. It may be necessary to 'look through' the holding structure to identify the real economic risks involved.

For example, suppose a UK company has a subsidiary in West Germany and that subsidiary has a French franc exposure. Let us further suppose that, because of a French franc devaluation, it loses DMarks 20,000. The UK parent company can expect to receive approximately DMarks 10,000 less after tax than before.

So the parent company's 'DM Dividends Receivable' item, which appears to be a DMark asset, actually behaves as though it were in part a French franc asset. This fact will not be apparent from the parent company accounts alone.

This indirect form of exposure is sensitive to movements of both the DMark and the French franc versus sterling. Clearly there are two separate exposures here, a transaction exposure in Germany of French francs v DMark, and a translation exposure in the UK of sterling v DMark.

If translation exposure is felt to be a concern, the the UK parent can handle this by a single (grossed up for UK tax) forward contract. It is open to the company's overall style of operation, in respect of its degree of centralisation, whether the transaction exposure is covered centrally or locally in Germany. Local cover is simplest in principle and introduces no new complications. Cover by the UK parent has to be partly grossed up to reflect the differential between UK and German marginal tax rates if cover there is to be neutral after tax on a consolidated basis.

The factor required is $F = \dfrac{(1 - Rg)}{(1 - Ruk)}$

where Rg is the marginal tax rate in Germany
Ruk is the marginal tax rate in the UK.

*Example*

Assume

| | | |
|---|---|---|
| Rg | = 40% | |
| Ruk | = 52% | |
| Exposure | = | FF1,000,000 |
| Initial Rate | 1 DM = | 2 FF |
| Final Rate | 1 DM = | 3 FF |

$F = \dfrac{(1 - \cdot 4)}{(1 - \cdot 52)} = 1 \cdot 25$

| | |
|---|---:|
| DM value of Initial FF receivable position | 500,000 |
| DM value of Final FF receivable | 333,333 |
| Loss on receivable | (166,667) |
| German tax relief @ 40% | 66,667 |
| | |
| Net Loss | (100,000) |
| Initial value of FF forward contract | (625,000) |
| Final value of FF forward contract | (416,666) |
| Gain on forward contract | 208,336 |
| Less tax at 52% | (108,336) |
| | |
| Net Gain | 100,000 |
| Overall change | nil |

Again, whenever cover of a transaction exposure of this type is undertaken by another group company other than the one having the original exposure, cash flow effects become important, especially in a situation such as that above where the two companies are in different countries.

# 13 Treasury Organisation

We have seen in discussing translation exposure that it may be difficult to identify what the economic exposure actually is. Equally difficult decisions arise in the more everyday world of cash flow exposure management. This is all the more discouraging because cash flow exposure seems at first sight not so much simple as downright obvious. Stepping back to consider alternative definitions of exposure can initially seem to be perverse, an unnecessary complication occluding a simple situation. It is, however, necessary to test the logic, bearing in mind Murphy's Law:

'If anything can go wrong, it will'

and the accompanying corollary:

'The hidden flaw never remains hidden.'

There are three stages; deciding the appropriate definition of exposure (that is, what is to be included in the case of a particular firm), setting up a system to provide the data necessary to calculate this exposure, and deciding what to do about the resultant exposure.

## What is Economic Exposure?

Economic exposure can be very different from the 'accounting exposure' as derived from the conventions of financial accounting. Some elements of economic exposures do not show up in financial accounts at all, some apparent exposures shown in financial accounts may not have any real economic impact upon the company.

Let us start with a very simple situation and gradually add complications one at a time. If we consider the case where we have a company having one export order to sell goods in currency, the economic exposure is clear. If the currency in which the goods are invoiced appreciates, the company will make a gain, and if it depreciates, the company will suffer a loss. The amount, currency and duration of the exposure are all known and hedging can be achieved by one forward contract.

It should be noted that this exposure will not necessarily (or even usually) show up in financial accounts at the time it arises. The balance sheet shows where funds are today, not where they will be in the future. The exposure arises as soon as the order is taken but it will not show on financial accounts until after manufacture – when it becomes a 'receivable'. Whilst the goods are in process of manufacture they are most likely to be valued at cost, and the fact that a future receivable is exposed to currency movement will not show up.

Thus Treasurers must decide whether they are to simply consider receivables in reckoning exposure, or receivables plus the uninvoiced order book, or even that total plus the sum of orders likely to be placed during the balance of the next, say, three months.

If we are prepared to project ahead for three months, why not six, or twelve? The question of the time horizon is vital in deciding what we mean by cash flow exposure. For most companies exporting in currency, the exposure really only exists until there is an opportunity to change the price. The price is likely to reflect domestic cost levels and so, after an interval, compensate the company for exchange rate changes. This ability to adjust price to reflect exchange rate changes is the principal hedging mechanism of the exporting company. It means that in practice some exchange exposures may only exist in the very short run because the impact of a currency movement on the economics of the firm will only last until the product price can be changed.

It may be objected that companies cannot put up prices whenever they wish and that if there was an existing opportunity they would of course do so in any case. To see why companies do have this scope it helps to look at an example. Suppose a US supplier is selling goods to Italy in competition with local manufacturers. Let us also suppose that the inflation rate in Italy is 15% per annum and in the US 5% per annum. Our US supplier will be able to increase his lira price by about 15% each year and still be competitive with local manufacture.

Equally, he will require to increase his prices by at least 5% measured in dollars to allow for his increased US costs. He can only continue to supply the Italian market on a profitable basis if the lira falls by no more than 10% per annum relative to the dollar. Fortunately, it can be demonstrated by statistical economists that *on average over a period of years* exchange rates do in fact move to compensate for inflation differentials fairly closely.

But averages are dangerous things. According to statistics if you stand with one foot in a bucket of boiling water and the other in a deep freeze, on average you are comfortable. Unfortunately, currency movements in the short run may differ widely from their expected long run trend. For this reason, short run economic exposure remains as a problem for the Treasurers, even if the company may reasonably hope that pricing can take care of the longer run shifts in the basic economics. The dilemma of course is that when things are going wrong in the short run, the long run may seem too far away to matter.

More subtle exposure problems arise if we now look at the above example from the point of view of the Italian importer. He seems to have no exchange risks at all, because he is invoiced in lira. He will certainly have no exposure showing on his financial accounts. Yet the price he pays over the longer term must move in line with the US dollar exchange rate because his supplier's costs are in dollars. It is as if his lira price is indexed (possibly with a lag) to the dollar. Only in the short run, until the next price increase, is his exposure genuinely zero. More generally, any source of supply represents a hidden currency risk to the firm in the currency of the supplier. Its duration may be considered to be the time required to arrange alternative sources of supply. A logical extension of these ideas, seldom explored by most companies because of the practical difficulties of getting the facts together, is that even local suppliers may represent an indirect currency exposure to the firm to the extent that in their turn they are supplied from abroad.

For most firms the source of supply will normally be chosen on considerations of quality, delivery or continuity of supply. Exchange exposure, particularly of this indirect variety, will have little influence on the firm's purchasing decision. It has to be managed after the event.

In precisely the same way as we considered when looking at the exposure existing on receivables, exposure on payables is likely to exceed the payables figure taken from the financial accounts. Items ordered and not yet invoiced, items due to be ordered, all may be taken into account when reckoning exposure.

## Collecting the Data

It is usually necessary to set up a separate data-gathering system for exposure management additional to the normal financial accounting data already available within the firm. This need not necessarily be particularly complex, but it is as well to realise that all of the data needed is not usually going to be available from the existing accounting system.

Reporting systems inevitably vary widely from firm to firm and almost invariably are tailor-made to the particular trading requirements of the firm concerned. Certain key ingredients are, however, common to most systems.

 a: Cash position by currency:
 cash at banks
 short term borrowings drawn
 undrawn facilities

 b: Future cash flow by currency, usually in monthly columns out to three months, thereafter quarterly:
 committed receipts
 committed disbursements
 estimated receipts
 estimated disbursements
 indirect exposures (foreign supplies, etc.)

 c: Forward cover taken.

 d: Net position by maturity, possibly with preset limits on this figure.

This internal data is usually supplemented by external, market, data concerning current interest rates and spot and outright foreign exchange rates. All the data is reviewed on a regular basis by some small group of people formed for the purpose. This team should include members from both the purchasing and sales sides of the business as well as treasury people, so that a two-way flow of ideas can be facilitated in this area. Most of all, the team should stay the same, so that all can learn from experience together and build up expertise. Some aspects of this process of building up the requisite experience were described in the later sections of Chapter 11 when discussing selective cover techniques.

As with anything else, it is helpful if the responsibilities and authority of the group are set out clearly in advance and if they in turn set clear limits as to the authority of the treasury staff who are to carry out the transactions. Here clarity of purpose must be paramount; elegant nuances aimed at 'flexibility' will only fudge important issues.

**Subsidiaries**

So far we have considered the situation of a single company trading only with third parties and having no domestic or foreign subsidiaries. We now introduce the complications that can arise for the Corporate Treasurer handling a group consisting of a parent company having one or more operating units or subsidiaries.

The first decision the group has to make is whether the group is to act as one in treasury matters, whether each company is to proceed as if the others did not exist, or whether to adopt some intermediate policy. The usual advantages and disadvantages of centralisation apply and the balance of these will be different in different industries and according to different styles of management. It is perhaps worth saying that over the last ten years there has been increased emphasis on centralising treasury decisions and very little evidence of moves to decentralise them, even where a company has been decentralising in other respects.

Where a group is entirely decentralised no new problems arise. Each company simply proceeds as if the other members of the group do not exist. Even at this level it is possible to arrange simple cost savings on foreign exchange deals by a little mutual planning. When goods are moving from one country to another, somebody has to do an exchange deal. Where the trading is between two members of the same group of companies, it may well pay them to agree that the currency risk, and therefore the currency deal to eliminate that risk, shall be done in the country which has the most developed foreign exchange market, so that the overall cost incurred between both parties is at a minimum. For instance, a UK company exporting to its subsidiary in Sweden would, other things being equal, be well advised to invoice in Swedish kronor so that the Swedish kronor/sterling transaction could be done in the large London foreign exchange market rather than in the higher margin market in Sweden.

Some companies have reached a halfway house whereby they split out decisions about translation exposure from those about cash flow exposure. Translation exposure is treated, as probably it has to be, as a 'group' matter, and hedging decisions are taken at Head Office. Such decisions may be regarded as directed towards protecting the future stream of earnings of the group. On the other hand protection of the current stream of earnings may be considered better handled where it arises, at the local level. In more decentralised groups this basis is consistent with the overall management style in the broader sense, and is often highly successful.

However, when it is felt worthwhile to centralise decisions more generally, for instance so that one company is not selling DMarks on the same day another company is buying them, some reporting and monitoring system has to be introduced.

The simplest way is for each company to deal small amounts in the same way as before but that each be required to ask the central treasury to handle all deals over a specified size. Proposed new commercial contracts in a foreign currency over a certain size limit are also referred to the central treasury before final signature. The degree of centralisation can then be altered simply by changing the cut off point at which the deals must be referred to the centre according to the level found to be economic by the company. Too many small deals in the centre simply create a lot of paper work and no great benefit. The benefits from centralisation arise both from the ability of the centre to net off exposures company against company and only deal in the market for the net amounts, and the ability to gross up exposures in one currency from several of the operating companies and do one large deal in the market. A large deal will normally command a better price than two or three small ones.

A variation of this idea is for the central company to offer forward cover at market rates to its other operating units. The individual operating units thus retain their autonomy to make their own decisions as to whether to cover, and the economics of their decisions are reflected in their local accounts. However, these inter-company deals booked within the group do not alter group exposure. The central treasury is still making the decision whether or not to cover this exposure with the market and thus alter the group exposure picture.

Where the subsidiary companies are relatively minor compared with the top company in the group, they may simply be asked to report their exposure to the top company which can then balance up the group exposure as it sees fit without requiring any action of any kind by the subsidiaries.

A neglected aspect of a centralised currency treasury operation is that it may well be that no single company in the group would be able to justify the cost of hiring staff with the necessary expertise, but that it may start to make sense if one central professional staff can handle the currency exposure for the whole group. In the longer run, the principal benefit the company may derive from centralisation may stem from the existence of this specialist team steadily acquiring expertise and contacts with the banking community. The general advice that this team can provide to the company can sometimes avoid expensive business decisions.

### MORE FORMALISED CENTRALISATION

Some companies have found it useful to set up much more formal arrangements to identify and monitor their cash flow exposure. There are as many different systems in use as those who have designed them – they have usually been 'custom built' by a gradual trial and error process. A fairly strict discipline is necessary for these systems to work since, as in other fields of 'Management Accounting', the facts have to be in consistent format, accurate and on time.

A typical such system might work as follows:

- *a*: Any group operating unit or domestic subsidiary *must* cover all foreign exchange exposure with the central treasury.

- *b*: Rates of exchange will be the middle market rate for the currency concerned for a three month forward outright deal. These prices will be set monthly and will then be held by the central treasury for one month ahead.

- *c*: The various operating units are now held accountable for the results of their commercial activities only, having no foreign exchange exposures.

- *d*: The central treasury may decide whether or not to cover the resultant net exposure as it thinks fit. If it were to cover all deals it should break even; if it is successful in selective cover, it will accrue a profit on these financial operations. (We consider later on how the central operation can attempt to analyse whether or not to cover.)

The effect of all this is of course to separate out responsibility as between commercial decisions and foreign exchange market decisions, whilst retaining the advantages of dealing for net amounts in the market. The cost savings inherent in dealing for say DMarks 500,000 as a purchase deal compared with selling DMarks 4 million and then buying back DMarks 4·5 million can be substantial. They are at the very least the difference between the market buying price and the market selling price for DMarks on the amount of DMarks 4 million, even ignoring the probability that the two deals might otherwise have been transacted on different days with the possibility of a rate movement in the interim. Usually there will be other minor cost savings in banking commissions and telex charges for transferring funds as well.

## DANGERS IN NETTING

It is necessary to exercise some care in netting off exchange exposures between companies in that the tax position of all subsidiaries may not be the same. This is especially necessary if some of the subsidiaries are in different countries since the tax treatment of exchange gains and losses is not uniform between countries. In this situation it is necessary to do some simple analysis of the effect on the group *after all taxes* of receiving an extra dollar of exchange gain in each company, or of incurring an extra dollar of exchange loss in each company. Only then can it be seen whether pre-tax netting will achieve a neutral post-tax result. It may be found that netting is only neutral as between certain of the group members and if so only their cash flows should be input to the netting system. Otherwise a real loss (and an after-tax exposure) will be created whenever the gain in one company is taxable and the corresponding loss in another is not allowable against tax at the same rate – or worse still, not allowable at all.

Enthusiasm for netting can also create local cash crises as it often works out that some unfortunate small subsidiary regularly collects an exchange loss. It may be desirable in these circumstances to allow one company to buy a currency and another to sell to allow a relatively illiquid group member to make an exchange gain.

Where the marginal tax rate differs between the two countries concerned it may be possible both to replenish the cash drain otherwise caused by netting and make an after-tax profit for the group. The top company may decide to invoice its foreign subsidiary either in a weak or a strong currency depending upon the relative marginal tax rate in the two countries. It being assumed that as an inter-company trade no overall exposure is created for the company, no cover will be taken out. As the exchange rate changes, the company in the low tax area will accrue a foreign exchange gain and the company in the high tax area incur a loss, thus creating a net profit to the group after tax. This is of course simply a variation on the well known theme of transfer pricing.

### Invoicing Companies

Some multinational groups have carried centralisation concepts further and have turned what we have called the 'central treasury' into an independent company. Here the rules for those parts of the group who are participating (normally only those 100% owned and having reasonably substantial exports or imports) are a little different. Such as:

> a: *For trading within the group*
> All companies must invoice exports destined for other group members to 'Invoice Co.' in their own currency. 'Invoice Co.' will charge on to the recipient company in the recipient's own currency. Thus neither the exporter of the goods nor the recipient of the goods will have any exchange risk.

> b: *For trading with third parties*
> Exports outside the group must either be invoiced to the customer in the exporting company's own currency or, if this is not acceptable, then it must again be invoiced to 'Invoice Co.' in the same currency. 'Invoice Co.' will invoice on to the customer in the agreed other currency.
> Similarly for imports, where again the only group company with an exchange risk is 'Invoice Co'.

> c: *Responsibilities of Invoice Co.*
> Since 'Invoice Co.' becomes the legal owner of the goods under this arrangement, it will normally have no problems in obtaining Exchange Control permission to do the necessary deals even in countries with very strict Exchange Control regimes. For the same reason such companies are often suitable vehicles for raising short term finance against receivables.

Different companies of this type have differing priorities but typical responsibilities and aims would include:

  i Monitoring group foreign exchange exposure, and taking appropriate decisions as to timing and extent of cover.

  ii Ensuring reporting procedures for the above are adequately set up and adhered to.

  iii Endeavouring by netting and otherwise to reduce the transaction and cash transfer costs of the group.

If all this is to work properly then each participant in the system must supply detailed forecasts for exports and imports split geographically so that Invoice Co. can calculate how the groups' exposure picture is changing. Supposing this daunting task has been accomplished and Invoice Co. is duly receiving both invoice notifications and forecasts, then it is still left with the problem of what to do about the net exposure pattern thus shown up. For each particular exposure it has to decide whether to cover, or not.

# 14 Currency Exchange Agreements (CEAs)

Following the publication of FASB 8 at the end of 1975 many US corporations started to look for new ways to hedge currency exposure over the medium term period, say five to fifteen years ahead. Some corporations had already studied this area in outline, but FASB 8 undoubtedly gave an added sense of urgency to the development of medium term techniques. Unfortunately, the normal foreign exchange market, geared as it is to the short term cover typical of current trade requirements, is quite unsuitable for this kind of longer term cover; as we have seen, for most currencies the market effectively dwindles to nothing beyond one or two years.

So attention first turned to the Eurocurrency markets which were then the only significant source of medium term currency funds. Not that most of these companies actually sought a source of funds *per se*, often they were liquid enough in their home currency. Ideally they sought to lend their home currency in return for a loan to them of a particular foreign currency and so balance up their FASB 8 exposure. This chapter examines the ways in which this objective has been achieved, initially by various forms of 'back-to-back' loans and then, in more recent years, by various versions of true 'Currency Exchange Agreements' or CEAs. For the purposes of illustration we will consider throughout the situation of an American corporation 'A Inc.' having dollars to lend and wishing to borrow sterling, and a British counterpart 'B Ltd' with the reverse situation. 'A Inc.' has a subsidiary in the UK that we shall call 'A Ltd' and similarly 'B Ltd' has a subsidiary in the US that we shall call 'B Inc.'.

The illustration is chosen solely because the dollar/sterling version of these transactions has been the one most frequently carried out; many other currency combinations are also regularly transacted.

**Back-to-Back Loans**

As with any new technique in any field, the innocent enquirer is immediately confronted with a mass of opaque and often quite unnecessary jargon. Let us dispose of this first. Back-to-back loans, reciprocal loans, paired loans, are all terms used to denote two loans in different currencies made reciprocally between the same counterparties. Thus A lends B dollars and B lends A sterling. Within this overall classification there are two essentially different mechanisms used, known as parallel loans and swap loans respectively. These we now take in turn:

PARALLEL LOANS

Parallel loans are used to arrange loans to each counterparty's subsidiary as illustrated below.

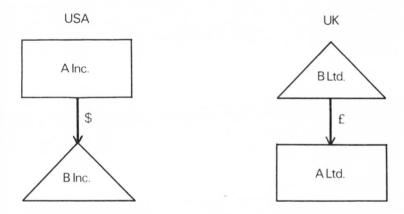

Here 'A Inc.' lends dollars to 'B Ltd's' US subsidiary, and 'B Ltd' lends sterling to 'A Inc.'s' UK subsidiary. From the point of view of 'A Inc.', its UK asset 'A Ltd' is now directly hedged by the sterling loan from 'B Ltd' and so the FASB 8 exposure is reduced.

The distinctive feature of this type of arrangement is that no funds flow across national borders. This enables parallel loans to be transacted even in certain strict Exchange Control environments. To this extent it can be a useful means to put otherwise inaccessible funds to use for the company in those cases where it is either disadvantageous or actually impossible to take funds out of a particular country. The funds may be used to collateralise another loan in a country where funds are required; the 'blocked' funds being lent to another company locally. There are, however, limitations on the extent to which this is possible in particular countries where central bank regulations may for instance preclude lending local currency to a foreign-owned subsidiary. It has to be checked out in each case.

## SWAP LOANS

Swap loans involve a different principle. Funds are exchanged directly between the two parties to the deal as shown below.

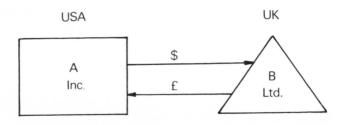

In countries having a system of Exchange Control, permissions will be required for the cross border transfer of funds at the commencement of the deal, and of course for those subsequent flows arising from interest instalments and eventual repayment. These difficulties do not currently arise in the case of UK/US transactions, such as that shown in our example.

Each loan serves as a collateral for the other, and the loan agreement between the parties will normally provide for a mutual right of set off. It may or may not include 'top-up' clauses to adjust the principal amounts in the light of future exchange rate movements in order to maintain collateral at or close to original levels. Set off arrangements are not possible with parallel loans. Because of the element of credit risk involved, only substantial, virtually 'undoubted' names are suitable candidates for swap or parallel loans, although greater latitude may be possible if one party is a bank and the other is a customer very well known to its banker.

COST STRUCTURE

Tax considerations usually preclude net interest payments on back-to-back deals. Full interest rates are thus charged on both loans at whatever rates the parties can mutually agree. Often this question is approached by setting a nominal, but market related, rate to the dollar side of the transaction and then negotiating about the appropriate differential that shall apply to the second currency. Forward premia on shorter periods or bond yields in the second currency (where they exist) may help to establish a rational basis for the second interest rate. As often as not it ends up as a leap in the dark and becomes simply a matter of what the two parties can live with.

Some arrangements are made at rates fixed for the entire life of the deal, some at fixed differential but with actual rates both ways varying in line with some key market rate for six months at a time. For instance, dollars to be lent at Eurodollar market six month LIBOR determined every six months, sterling to be lent at this rate plus 2% per annum. Some deals even allow both rates to vary in line with their respective market rates, setting say dollars at LIBOR as above and sterling at say MLR + 1% per annum.

This method of calculating cost is usually considered more appropriate in those cases where the transaction is made for a variable period, rather than for a fixed period. That is, a deal may be made for a period variable between five and ten years so that, after the expiry of the first five years, either party may call for termination of the deal by giving six months notice, and that notice is binding on the other party.

Where the two parties are introduced to each other and the deal arranged by a bank, the bank will charge a fee as a percentage of the size of the transaction. Such a fee may be either once only or payable annually during the life of the transaction.


LIMITATIONS

Back-to-back loans achieve their objectives reliably and reasonably simply. They do hedge exposure in fact and in terms of the various national accounting conventions – FASB 8, ED 21, etc. They do manage to do this for longer periods than the foreign exchange market can handle. But the arrangements for set-off and counter-party risk can be cumbersome in practice, and both sides of the deal show on the balance sheet, raising gearing and limiting both parties' ability to raise other finance for quite a long period ahead.

Parallel loans remain in many cases as the only possible way to solve a problem, but swap loans are now increasingly replaced by a more recent, derived alternative, the Currency Exchange Agreement, or CEA.

## Currency Exchange Agreements

It is apparent that the swap loan agreement is theoretically exactly equivalent to an initial exchange transaction between the parties, with a second, reversing exchange transaction at maturity. Setting up the arrangement in this manner enables it to become 'off-balance sheet' and avoids the gearing and other implications of the swap loan technique. Consequently CEAs have increasingly come to replace swap loan arrangements. CEAs themselves have evolved into several different forms, basically variants on three different models.

### SIMPLE CEA

The two companies enter into an agreement providing for actual exchange currencies on the start date at market rates, conditional upon eventual re-exchange *at the same rate* on a specified future date, say seven years hence, irrespective of the market exchange rate at that time.

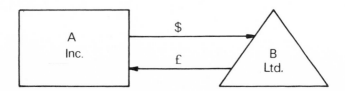

On the re-exchange date actual funds are duly put up and transferred to the other party, so achieving the same net effect as by the swap loan method.

INITIAL EXCHANGE NOTIONAL

A simplification is achievable, and also one cumbersome transfer of the funds is thereby eliminated, if the parties agree that they shall *deem* that the initial exchange has been made and that the re-exchange shall take place as if it had. Clearly each company is able to obtain the initial countervalue in the other currency by direct deal in the foreign exchange market if it requires it without involving the other party at all. The objective of the CEA from the companies' point of view is solely to secure the eventual re-exchange. In some countries an actual initial exchange may be compulsory as a condition of Exchange Control permission for the CEA, or there may be tax or Accounting Exposure reason for actual initial exchange. Each company must check this for themselves.

NET RE-EXCHANGE ONLY

The besetting problem of all back-to-back loans or CEAs is the credit risk. Amounts tend to be substantial, say from ten million dollars upwards, and maturities anywhere from five to fifteen years. Any means to reduce the credit risk faced by the two parties is thus of great significance. A major improvement is achievable if the credit risk can be reduced from the full gross amount of the transaction, to the net difference between the two eventual money amounts at maturity. For example:

|   |   | Initial Date | Re-exchange Date |
|---|---|---|---|
| 1 | £ amount dealt | £10,000,000 | £10,000,000 |
| 2 | Exchange rate | 2.00 | 1.50 |
| 3 | $ market value of sterling | $20,000,000 | £15,000,000 |
| 4 | $ amount dealt = gross credit risk | $20,000,000 | $20,000,000 |
| 5 | Net dollar debt = net credit risk | nil | $5,000,000 |

Therefore some CEAs have provisions for only the net payment (here five million dollars) to be made at maturity, rather than requiring actual payments of ten million pounds and twenty million dollars respectively. In the event of default, the credit risk is reduced. Unfortunately, this route is also frequently barred by Exchange Control, tax or Accounting Exposure considerations, in which case the parties concerned revert to the simple CEA with actual gross transfers of funds at start and finish. In this event credit risk may still be reducible to the net by arranging for a bank or banks to act as stakeholders at maturity, only paying away any funds when both payments have been received. The appendix to this chapter sets out the payment mechanics in more detail.

COST STRUCTURE

Cost structure can be identical to that discussed under back-to-back loans. However, in the case of CEAs it is also possible to pay the agreed interest differential only, rather than for each side to pay interest gross to the other. Accounting and tax practice will then consider the interest differential to be a 'fee'. It follows after all that the fee cannot be interest as technically there are no loans in existence. Depending on the exact circumstances, there may or may not be a tax advantage in choosing one cost basis rather than the other.

APPENDIX

**Mechanics**

The actual mechanics of the exchange of currencies at the start and maturity of either back-to-back loans or CEAs are identical. They can also be surprisingly complex owing to the need to ensure that both loans are begun (and repaid) simultaneously so as to avoid the possibility of an uncovered credit risk for either party. We now consider these mechanics in detail, first assuming that one counterparty is itself a bank, and then assuming that neither counterparty is a bank.

*Example* 1
Most CEAs so far transacted have a bank as one of the counterparties. In this first example we will assume that this is the case and also that the bank concerned has offices in both London and New York. It is immaterial whether it is a New York bank with a London branch or whether it is a London bank with a New York branch or indeed is say a French bank with branches in both cities. We will further assume that the bank is the provider of dollars. 'A

Inc.' thus becomes 'A Bank'. The procedure for the first exchange is then:

1. 'B Ltd' puts up £Xm at the London branch of 'A Bank'. Deadline: 2 p.m. London time.

2. The 'Reference Bank', 'R Bank', advises both parties the middle spot rate existing 2 days previously at say 11 a.m. London time; that is, the spot rate that would provide exchange today. This rate fixes the dollar countervalue required. Since 'A Bank' has a vested interest in the rate itself, it is usual to ask an independent bank to act as a Reference Bank in this way.

3. Subject to step 1 having taken place 'A Bank's' New York branch pays the $ countervalue to 'B Ltd's' own bankers in New York. Deadline: 11 a.m. New York time.

Similar arrangements apply at the time of the eventual re exchange.


*Example 2*

The above example was relatively straightforward owing to the assumption that one of the counterparties, 'A Bank', was considered undoubted as a credit risk. Where two commercial companies are the counterparties more safeguards would be customary in carrying out the exchange, each party using their own bankers as 'stakeholders' with conditional payment instructions to pass funds on to the counterparty's stakeholder bank. Up to five banks may thus become involved in the exchange, although one bank may often assume more than one role in the transaction, so reducing the number involved. The five roles are:

   i The Reference Bank, as before, 'R Bank'

   ii 'A Inc.'s' bankers in New York, 'A NY'.

   iii 'A Inc.'s' bankers in London, 'A L'.

   iv 'B Ltd's' bankers in New York, 'B NY'.

   v 'B Ltd's' bankers in London, 'B L'.

The steps to be carried out are illustrated on page 133 and may be set out as follows:

1. 'B Ltd' puts up £Xm at its London bankers, 'B L'. The funds are placed on a specially designated account and are accompanied by a conditional payment order on the following lines.

To: 'B L'

Dear Sirs,

(i) We hereby irrevocably instruct you to transfer £Xm on deposit with you in our special account (Account No.          ) to the special account of A Inc. with 'A L' (Account No.          ), such transfer to be made on or after 23 November 1980, as soon as you have received notification from 'A NY' that it is holding on deposit $Ym subject to irrevocable instructions (accepted in the terms endorsed thereon) to transfer such deposit to our special account with 'B NY' upon receipt from you of notification that you are holding £Xm subject to the instructions contained in this letter and the acceptance endorsed on it.

(ii) Please acknowledge receipt and acceptance of these instructions in the space provided on the enclosed copy of this letter and immediately inform 'A NY' that you are holding £Xm subject to the instructions contained in this letter and the acceptance endorsed on it.

(iii) If you do not receive the notification from 'A NY' referred to in paragraph 1 hereof on or before 12 noon New York time on 23 November 1980, these instructions shall become void and the £Xm mentioned in these instructions shall remain on deposit in our special account subject to our further instructions.

Deadline for this: 10 a.m. London time.

2. 'B L' advises 'A NY' that it now has the sterling available subject to the conditional order.

3. The Reference Bank 'R Bank', advises both parties and 'A NY' the middle spot rate existing 2 days previously, as in *Example* 1. This fixes the $ countervalue as say $Ym.

USA

UK

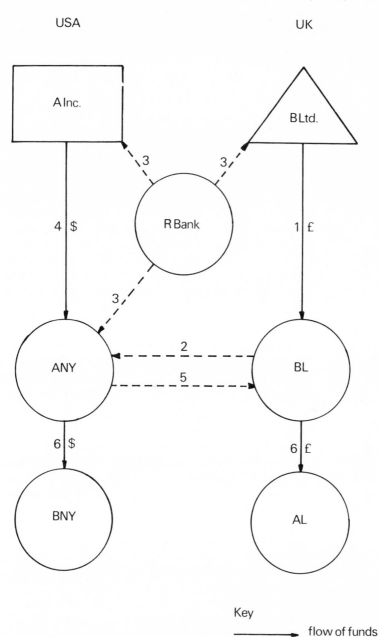

Key

——————▶ flow of funds

— — — ▶ telex advice

4. 'A Inc.' puts up $Ym at its New York bankers, 'A NY'. The funds are placed on a specially designated account and are accompanied by a conditional payment order on the following lines.

To 'A NY'

Dear Sirs,

(i) We hereby irrevocably instruct you to transfer $Ym on deposit with you in our special account (Account No.          ) to the special account of 'B Ltd' with 'B NY' (Account No.          ) such transfer to be made on or after 23 November 1980 as soon as you have received notification from 'B L' that it is holding on deposit £Xm subject to irrevocable instructions (accepted in the terms endorsed thereon) to transfer such deposit to our special account with 'A L' upon receipt from you of notification that you are holding $Ym subject to the instructions contained in this letter and the acceptance endorsed on it.

(ii) Please acknowledge receipt and acceptance of these instructions in the space provided on the enclosed copy of this letter and immediately inform 'B L' that you are holding $Ym subject to the instructions contained in this letter and the acceptance endorsed on it.

(iii) If you do not receive the notification from 'B L' referred to in paragraph 1 hereof on or before 12 noon New York time on 23 November 1980, these instructions shall become void and the $Ym mentioned in these instructions shall remain on deposit in our special account subject to our further instructions.

Deadline for this: 10 a.m. New York time.

5. 'A NY' advises 'B L' that it now has the dollars available subject to the conditional order and that it has received 'B L's' advice from step 2.

6. The conditions now being satisfied, 'A NY' pays $Ym to 'B NY' and 'B L' pays £Xm to 'A L'.

# 15 Forecasting Exchange Rates

Any attempt to predict the future necessarily has its limitations, and this is certainly true in the area of exchange rate forecasts. Nevertheless, imperfect though our techniques are, they can provide a worthwhile degree of help in our efforts to peer into the crystal ball. As more economists and others take up this subject as a field of study, perhaps techniques will improve. Even if they do, however, accuracy may not get better – when everyone is 'one step ahead', each individual's net advantage in seeking to out-guess the market remains nil; and, as stock market analysts have found, the principal result is that the market discounts expected changes more rapidly.

Despite this gloomy beginning, it should not be assumed that forecasting is either pointless or likely to mislead as often as predict. After all, many participants in the market do not bother to concern themselves about the outlook but simply deal spot when payments are due. Others operate a company policy of covering forward at all times, so that their actions do not reflect changes in the outlook either. Yet others assiduously read the forecasts drawn up by their economists or bankers but take no action as a result. So those that take the trouble to draw up forecasts and use them as a guide to action are at an advantage.

## A Framework

Before launching into long economic arguments, it is well to go briefly back to basics. Foreign exchange rates are simple prices, whose level is dictated by supply and demand. In turn the net cash flow moving across the foreign exchange market may be thought of as made up from:
- *capital movements*
    for long term investments, dividend flow, arbitrage or speculation, and central bank intervention;

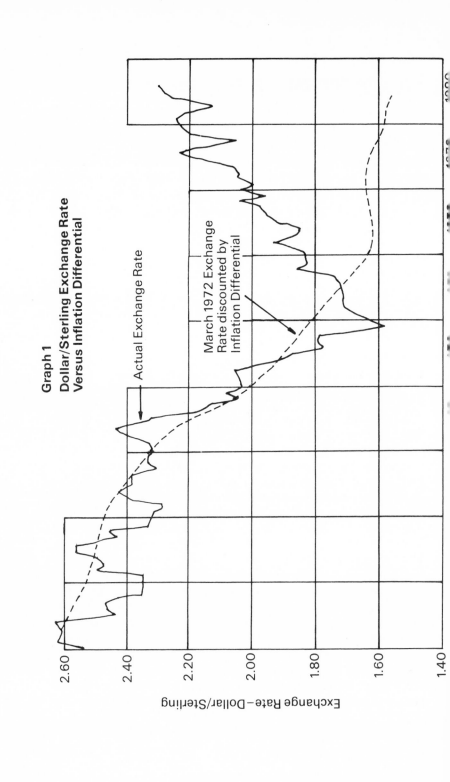

**Graph 1**
**Dollar/Sterling Exchange Rate Versus Inflation Differential**

Actual Exchange Rate

March 1972 Exchange Rate discounted by Inflation Differential

Exchange Rate—Dollar/Sterling

2.60
2.40
2.20
2.00
1.80
1.60
1.40

- *ordinary trade*
  exports and imports, net receipts from tourism, etc.;
- *trade in commodities*
  oil and gas, metals and ores, and staple foodstuffs.

Some of these money flows will be highly responsive to changes in the economic outlook for the country concerned, others radically less so. Some, such as those resulting from intervention policy, determined by the central bank, are probably not material in the long run, but dominant on a day to day market basis. The criteria relevant to our forecast depend upon the time period in question.

Thus armed, we can advance cautiously into a consideration of the factors influencing exchange rates. If we can identify these factors and predict their future course, then we can forecast exchange rates. We shall handle these influences in three categories:

- long run influences
- short run influences
- day to day influences

## Long Run Influences

The 'long run' is considered as a period of several years over which a trend can be established which over-rides the fluctuations which occur in the short run.

Exchange rate forecasting may be approached in two ways, depending upon whether the shorter or longer term outcome is of more concern to the forecaster. If the long run is important but the shorter term less so, then the appropriate forecasting technique is to establish long run trends from historical data and look for economic factors that correlate with the trend, and then use these 'proxy variables' to predict the future course of the trend line. Shorter term movements above or below the trend line will be of less concern except in seeking to establish confidence limits for forecasts (e.g. if in the past short run movements have rarely caused actual rates to move more than 5% away from the trend line then future rates would also be expected to be within ±5% of a correctly forecast trend line).

The most widely known long run influence is inflation. This is demonstrated in Graph 1 which shows the case of the dollar/sterling exchange rate. The graph shows the actual path taken by the exchange rate, together with a line showing the effect of discounting the exchange rate as it existed on 31 March 1972 by the annual difference between UK and US inflation rates. (So if inflation was 8% higher in the UK than in the US in a given year, the line would fall 8% in the year.) The initial correspondence between the two lines is striking.

It is nevertheless true that a blind follower of the 'inflation index' would have found his forecast seriously astray in individual years. For instance, at the end of 1974 the actual rate was showing appreciably above 'trend' yet continued to rise for a full six months before plunging some 25 cents to the trend line.

Worse, seen in the early years the good general correlation observed here only remains true 'other things being equal', and other things are not always equal. In the case of the UK, the emergence of a totally new factor in the shape of North Sea oil revenues has effectively destroyed the usefulness of inflation alone as a predictor of exchange rates. Graph 1 can be regarded as a rough estimate of where sterling would have moved to had there been no North Sea oil.

But where no substantial new factors come onto the scene, inflation differentials can be a very good guide to exchange rate movements in the long run. This has held true for all the major European currencies against the dollar (and of course against each other) during the seventies. Thus, although the DMark had appreciated by some 22% against the dollar in the years 1973–76, some 20% of this was 'accounted for' by the inflation differential. In the same period the Italian lira fell by some 27% against the dollar, of which about 24% was 'accounted for' by the inflation differential.

It is of course statistically more accurate to consider the overall level of each currency against all other currencies, rather than just a single exchange rate against some key currency, such as the dollar. The level of any one currency is likely to be influenced by the performance of all its major trading partners rather than just one of these. If the dollar/sterling rate moves from $2.40 to $2.10 did sterling fall or did the dollar rise?

The normal way out of these two problems is to reckon the level of each currency on an index basis against a trade-weighted basket of its principal trading partners – the 'effective exchange rate'.

This index would be expected to correlate with the inflation differential between the country concerned and its trading partners. That is, if the inflation differential is such that France is experiencing an inflation rate 4% per annum in excess of the average of its trading partners then it would be expected that the Effective Exchange Rate for the French franc would fall by 4% per annum also.

Proceeding one further step, the Effective Exchange Rate discounted for inflation differential, or 'Real Effective Exchange Rate', might be expected to remain roughly constant over time. But does it? The table below shows the statistics from 1973 to 1980 for a number of major currencies. It is striking that, with the exception of the UK after the impact of North Sea oil, movements in Real Effective Exchange Rate are not only relatively small, but also tend to come back towards the parity level of 100 given a long enough time period. This somewhat more sophisticated analysis confirms the earlier broad conclusion that inflation differential is a good long run predictor so long as nothing too radical occurs to alter a country's existing pattern of external trade.

### Real Effective Exchange Rates

Index numbers, March 1973 = 100. The index of the Real Effective Exchange Rate is the index of the effective exchange rate adjusted for inflation differentials which are measured by wholesale prices of nonfood manufactures. Exchange rates and trade weights used in the construction of this index are the same as those used for effective exchange rate indices. Annual figures are averages of months.

|         | 1974  | 1975  | 1976  | 1977  | 1978  | 1979  | 1980* |
|---------|-------|-------|-------|-------|-------|-------|-------|
| USA     | 95·1  | 98·6  | 100·3 | 100·0 | 95·4  | 95·5  | 99·4  |
| Canada  | 107·5 | 102·6 | 106·7 | 99·8  | 92·9  | 92·9  | 94·3  |
| UK      | 100·8 | 104·4 | 96·6  | 101·6 | 106·4 | 118·6 | 132·8 |
| Germany | 105·3 | 100·5 | 101·2 | 102·5 | 103·3 | 104·3 | 103·0 |
| France  | 94·7  | 102·6 | 100·0 | 96·1  | 96·8  | 98·6  | 99·3  |
| Italy   | 104·6 | 97·8  | 92·6  | 95·6  | 93·8  | 93·6  | 97·4  |
| Switz.  | 93·5  | 104·1 | 110·9 | 105·2 | 121·7 | 115·4 | 103·6 |
| Sweden  | 106·1 | 105·9 | 109·1 | 105·1 | 96·6  | 99·2  | 99·8  |

* Figure shown is for March 1980
Source: World Financial Markets
        Morgan Guaranty Trust Company of New York

Looking at the same result in another way, it may be said that for a few currencies, where the pattern of external trade is undergoing substantial change, the Real Effective Exchange Rate will exhibit a trend so that it gradually shifts its level over time. But for most currencies this trend line is virtually horizontal.

So, whether or not this trend line is horizontal for a given currency it can be used to provide a good longer term rate predictor.

But what causes the shorter term movements above and below the trend?


## Short Run Influences

If the main concern is to forecast rates in the shorter run, then the long run influences merely serve as background to a specifically short run forecast. There are a number of schools of thought as to the factors having most influence on exchange rates in the shorter run. The main arguments will be set out for each of them, and we leave it to economists to refine the ideas involved and to determine which of the arguments will prevail. For our purposes we must simply use the tools that come to hand, recognising that widespread public awareness of any forecasting theory can help to make the theory self fulfilling.

Theory 1: *Inflation is the Key Factor*
As we have seen, inflation differentials do provide a good correlation in the longer run in the absence of any new factors in the economy, but have not been a good predictor in the short run.

The main arguments for using inflation trends to predict exchange rate trends is that, in the competitive international markets of today, export prices tend to equate worldwide, otherwise countries encounter difficulties in their international trade. (For this reason, some economists prefer to use an index of export prices rather than the more widely based consumer price index when looking at these correlations.) The reasoning is that if a country is experiencing high inflation relative to competitor nations, its balance of payments will go into deficit because its exports will be priced out of world markets, whilst imports will become cheaper relative to locally produced goods. The resultant outward flow of money over the exchanges will tend to lower the exchange rate.

The argument contains the reason why inflation is not the ideal 'key factor' to choose – it really only works as a 'proxy' for estimating balance of payments outturns, and factors other than inflation influence balance of payments too.

### Theory 2: *Outlook for Inflation is the Key Factor*

This is a variation on the first idea, and has been advanced to provide a partial answer to the objection that exchange rate movements do not seem to correlate very well with levels of inflation in the shorter run. They do correlate a little better with changes in the outlook for inflation, but not much.

The argument is that because the broad relationship between exchange rates and inflation differentials has become widely realised by market operators, they tend to respond immediately to news likely to change the outlook for inflation, thus discounting the expected trend. So the rate may follow changes in inflationary expectations more closely than the actual level of inflation. The idea that expectations about inflation may be more relevant than actual current levels leads us directly into the monetary area.

It is now widely accepted that a major engine of inflation is excessive monetary growth. So that, working back through the logical chain to the source of the problem:

- The exchange rate is determined by sales and purchases in the market.
- A major source (usually *the* major source) of these transactions is the current account of the balance of payments.
- Inflation may be a good predictor of the balance of payments.
- Excessive monetary growth is a principal source of inflation.

So it seems sensible to see whether the rate of monetary growth is a good predictor.

### Theory 3: *Rate of Monetary Growth is the Key Factor*

Monetarist economists argue that, in an ideal world starting with zero inflation rates, money supply should only be allowed to expand to an extent equal to rate of growth of productive capacity in the economy. Any excess monetary growth beyond that simply provides an input to inflation.

Excess money supply might be regarded as a source of a depreciating exchange rate for a number of different reasons:

*a*: The extent of excess money supply is a prime determinant of future inflation rates, which themselves correlate approximately with exchange rate movements.

Since money supply changes precede changes in inflation, money supply changes may precede exchange rate changes and so be more useful as a predictor.

*b*: A more fundamental argument runs as follows. Consider what would happen in the event that a country unilaterally increases the money in circulation within its borders by a factor of, say, two. It must be expected that the outside world will soon come to value a unit of this currency at half the previous value, so as to keep the external value of that country's total money stock at a constant level.

No doubt there will also be rapid inflation within the country as prices accelerate towards (and possibly beyond) double their previous levels, but there is no certainty that this inflation will proceed at the same speed as the movement in the exchange rate.

On this view, inflation only correlates with exchange rates because both are determined by excess money supply. If the lags in the system are different for these two by-products, then excess money supply will correlate with exchange rates more closely than inflation will, although inflation would be expected to show the right general trend over time.

*c*: A different argument may be advanced by considering where the excess money supply will find its outlet. The excess money is by definition surplus to the requirements of the domestic economy. It is reasonable to argue that where the domestic supply of money exceeds the domestic demand for money, the excess must find its way out of the country. This flow of funds over the exchanges will represent a direct pressure on the exchange rate. The downward pressure on the exchange rates then increases the cost of imports and so adds to inflation.

There are a number of ways in which excess money supply might be measured. Perhaps the simplest is to use the most basic measure of money supply, 'M1'* (footnote on page 143), and look at its annual rate of increase.

As an initial illustration the figures for the UK for 1974 and 1975 are instructive:

|  | Year on Year Rates | |
|---|---|---|
|  | Mid 1974 | Mid 1975 |
| Growth in money supply (M1 % per annum) | 0·2 | + 19.7 |
| Inflation rate, % per annum | 16 | 25 |

It can be seen at once that in mid-1974 UK money supply was static, but that in mid-1975 it was exploding at an uncontrolled 19·7% per annum. On this evidence we would expect sterling to remain static or to improve somewhat in 1974 relative to other currencies but to fall steeply in 1975. Which is exactly what did happen.

Note also that if inflation really was the main determinant of exchange rates in the short term, then sterling should have fallen substantially in 1974 as well as in 1975.

Obtaining this crude result inevitably causes one to wonder whether changes in the money supply may be used as predictors of the 'wobbles' in Real Effective Exchange Rates apparent from the table on page 139. *A priori,* it would be expected that unusually tight or unusually relaxed monetary conditions for the country concerned would lead to temporary increases and decreases in Real Effective Exchange Rates, possibly with some degree of lag before the changed monetary climate fed through to the exchange rates.

---

* M1 is the narrow definition of 'money supply'. It comprises notes and coin in circulation plus money on current account at banks. It may be used as a 'proxy' for the general level of transactions in the economy. Its usefulness in this respect is constrained by two complicating factors:
  - Some short run changes in M1 stem from changes in interest rates. In periods of high interest rates people tend to keep balances on non-interest bearing accounts to a minimum, and place funds on fixed deposits, which are not included in M1.
  - over a period of years financial awareness is increasing as banks and other financial institutions offer alternative media for short term invest-ment, and faster methods of payment (such as credit cards). So a given level of M1 tends to permit a slightly larger turnover of transactions year by year. In the jargon, 'the velocity of circulation of money' is increasing.

**Graph 2**
**West Germany. Real Effective Exchange Rate & Money Supply**

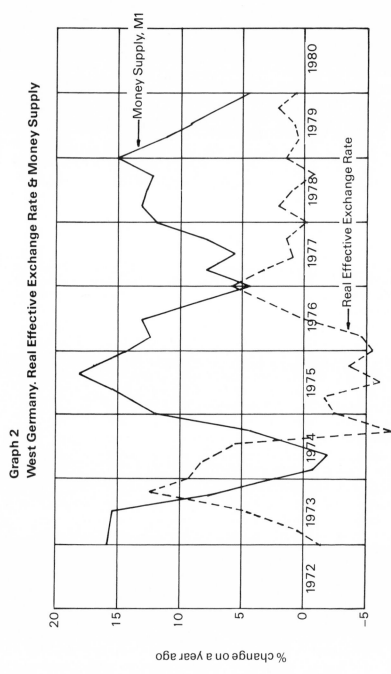

Source: Real Effective Exchange Rate, Morgan Guaranty
Changes in M1, Deutsche Bundesbank

The simplest test to apply is to plot actual changes in M1 and changes in Real Effective Exchange Rates on a common scale against time. The argument would lead us to expect that higher than average increases in M1 would be associated with falls in Real Effective Exchange Rate and vice versa. Graph 2 shows the two variables for the case of West Germany.

It being taken for granted that none of these exercises will ever give a perfect result – we are after all relying on massive over-simplification of a most complex environment – the relationship is surprisingly good.

A substantial part of the variation of Real Effective Exchange Rate about its long term trend line is thus seen to be 'explainable' by the money supply variation. But not all. The problem remains that all these methods are really no more than indirect predictors of the current account of the balance of payments – and only part of the balance of payments at that, namely that determined by international price competitiveness such as trade in manufactures. Throughout the mid-seventies the United Arab Emirates (UAE) had massive inflation of some 40 per cent per annum together with a rapidly increasing money supply. Yet, due to the impact of oil exports the current account was in surplus and the UAE dirham remained strong. Perhaps it will prove more reliable to go directly to predict the current account itself.

Theory 4: *The Current Account is the Key Factor*
This is the most longstanding of the many theories of influences on exchange rates.

The basic argument starts very solidly in that it states that an exchange rate, being the price which balances buyers and sellers of the currency, must be determined by all those cash flows moving through the foreign exchange market. For most countries the bulk of the money going over the exchanges arises from the regular net flow of payments and receipts for goods and services, and the net remittance of dividends and interest earned on investments. The net flow of money resulting from all these sources is the Current Account of the Balance of Payments.

A country with a current account in deficit will experience steady selling of its currency in the market to the extent of the deficit, thus depressing the rate. So some forecasters have developed very complex economic models to try to predict the outturn on current account as a means to predict exchange rates.

A particular difficulty with this forecasting approach lies in the fact that even for those economies where the current account correlates reasonably well with the exchange rate, changes in the current account tend to lag changes in the exchange rate rather than to lead it, so that the value of current account forecasts as prediction tools is diminished.

But the major problem with this approach is that the current account is only one element of the Balance of Payments. The other element is the capital account. Although it has proved possible to make sensible projections about the current account, the capital account remains as something of a leap in the dark for the forecaster.

The capital account is made up from the net movement of deposit and investment funds into or out of the country. Unfortunately, these flows have often been largely generated by changes in investors' perception of the outlook for the exchange rate, as in the heavy purchases of UK Government Bonds by continental investors in early 1977, or the similarly massive liquidation of foreign sterling holdings during 1976.

At this point the argument is circular, like the chicken and egg conundrum, so analysts have to make some assumption which will assist in estimating the capital account outturn.

Some analysts have endeavoured to convince themselves that these capital flows will usually reflect expectations about the trend of the current account, so that estimates of the trend of the current account will not only be useful in themselves but will also act as a proxy for the capital account movements.

Another approach to arriving at an estimate for the capital account is to assume that the outturn is determined by interest rate differentials. Relatively high interest rates can be expected to lead to capital inflows, lower rates to outflows. Even this picture is overlaid by bond investors who tend to come into a currency with high interest rates only when rates are expected to fall, so as to collect a profit on the increased market price of the bond when yields fall.

Work on this somewhat intractable area continues amongst the 'international monetarist' school of economists in Chicago and London as they continue to develop a comprehensive theory to explain and predict capital account movements. Perhaps this is the most likely source of a satisfactory prediction tool in the longer run.

As yet it can only be said that forecasting the outturn on capital account remains a hazardous art.

At least one major currency however, remains largely independent of the whims of international portfolio managers and is a reasonably reliable current account balance follower. It is the Japanese yen. Throughout the decade of the seventies changes in the dollar/yen exchange rate followed changes in the Japanese current account with great precision. In turn, changes in the current account mainly derived from changes in import levels rather than from the more stable pattern shown by exports. But the low level of capital transactions in yen probably made it a special case amongst the major currencies.

Theory 5: *Central Bank Policy is the Key*
Strictly speaking, all the various factors discussed above as methods of prediction of exchange rates are actually predictors of flows of funds over the exchanges. Whether these flows result in rate movements is dependent upon whether the central bank chooses to intervene to offset them. In the case of an outflow, the authorities have to decide whether to let the rate fall or whether to spend part of the country's currency reserves on intervention purchases to maintain the rate.

If a central bank decides upon a policy of intervention, then the most carefully researched forecasts are rendered useless. For instance, throughout the early 1970s Denmark had a consistent balance of payments deficit, a poor inflation record and a high rate of monetary growth. But the Danish krone remained a strong currency because the Central bank considered it a priority to maintain the existing parity within the Snake system (see Appendix A) and therefore consistently supported the currency. It was able to do this because Denmark was ready to top up its reserves from time to time by raising substantial foreign loans.

Where the policy of the central bank as to the desired future course of the exchange rate differs from the market's view of the prospects for the currency, forecasting becomes reduced to estimates of the policy decisions of the authorities and the extent to which they will be prepared to act to offset market pressures.

For instance, over the weekend of 29–30 October 1977, the Bank of England changed its policy from 'intervening to maintain a stable exchange rate' to 'temporary non-intervention'. During the first hour of trading on 31 October the sterling exchange rate against the dollar went from 1·77 to 1·84. This rate movement was greater than the total movement experienced over the previous six months.


*Followers*

The above theories are only genuinely valid for the currencies of the half dozen or so major world currencies. Other central banks are obliged to take into account the behaviour of the major units in setting target levels for their own currencies. Smaller currency markets are also more susceptible to direct central bank control and more directly reflect that policy. The Nordic currencies provide a typical example.

Given the limitations of market size, it has not been possible for Nordic currencies to adopt any policy of leadership, but instead they have sought various models of followership, whereby they can follow at one remove the movements of other more dominant currencies. Throughout the mid-seventies the main method used to follow the performance of other currencies was the European Snake. From the early days of the European Snake all three Scandinavian currencies entered into some form of membership, either as a direct member, as in the case of Denmark, or as associate members, as in the case of Norway and Sweden. Finland, as is usual in its international relationships, did not formally join the Snake but nevertheless shadowed the progress of the Snake keeping an eye on the cross rates for the Finnmark against the Snake currencies, but also taking account of the movement of other non-Snake currencies. So in this phase of development, the Nordic currencies followed the DMark. It was not entirely a success, due to the strength of the DMark at this time.

The Norwegian currency was obliged to strengthen in order to follow the DMark in the Snake. When the pressure on the domestic economy became too great, a devaluation would follow, putting the rate back more or less where it was before against the dollar. A graph of the Norwegian kroner during this period shows a sawtooth pattern, a rising slope, a vertical fall, a rising slope and then a vertical fall. The fact is that the Norwegian economy is quite heavily dependent upon dollar priced trade. Aligning Norway with the DMark dominated Snake could not disguise the fact for long; the trading pattern kept obstinately showing through and dictating the outcome. But forecasting during this period consisted only of predicting the size and date of the next realignment. Until then the krone would follow the DMark.

Because of the increasingly frequent and large devaluations measured against the DMark, a new solution had to be found. The fact that a lot of the devaluations were almost entirely illusory because they were being measured against the DMark, one of the strongest currencies in the world during the period, did not necessarily register with opinion at home. It seemed bad for national morale and politically damaging for governments to have to keep announcing devaluations.

From the outset Finland adopted a slightly different approach to the Scandinavian countries in that they were seeking to stabilise the value of their currency against a basket of their principal trading partners. This system was commenced as early as 1974 and remains in force today.

The mechanism allowed very gradual changes in the value of the Finnmark against particular currencies whilst enabling the value of the Finnmark to remain constant against the measure that mattered most to the Finnish economy, that is the average of their trading partners' currencies. Thus, although the Finnmark fell steadily against the DMark during this period, it also registered other gains, such as against the pound sterling, which compensated. Most of all at no time was any drama necessary in order to achieve these gradual changes. In due course both Sweden and Norway moved to a broadly similar system. Today Finland still uses her original basket concept, revising the weights of the individual constituent currencies from time to time to reflect the slowly changing pattern of her external trade. The weights are published in the excellent Suomen Pankki 'Monthly Bulletin', as are the current levels of the index and the fluctuation limits permitted, $\pm 2\frac{1}{4}\%$. The Sveriges Riksbank, and the Norges Bank, also publish both their basket makeup and the current level of their indices, but not the permitted fluctuation range.

Forecasting here consists of estimating the course of the constituent currencies and then calculating say, the Swedish krona v US dollar rate by simple arithmetic. Forecasts of economic variables are largely irrelevant except in so far as they may become so much out of line with broader Government objectives as to ultimately cause abandonment of the exchange rate policy.

**Relative Importance of These Theories**

As has been seen, each of the above theories can be very successful in the right circumstances; equally, each of them have basic limitations. Intense discussions about which theory is more 'correct' are inherently unhelpful to the working Treasurer, and also may be missing the point. Is it more correct to use a putter, a driver, or a five iron? It depends upon the circumstances at the time. What is required is some means to preselect which of the tools in the bag is the right one for the job, and use it in those circumstances only.

At the risk of gross oversimplification perhaps a look at the diagram on page 151 will clarify matters. Four sources of the flow of money across the foreign exchanges are identified. The first task is to form an opinion as to which of these can be expected to be dominant in the case of a particular currency at a particular time, and then to seek data or use forecasting theories most relevant to predicting that component. Clearly money supply and inflation-based forecasts are essentially estimates of Group 1, current account-based methods attempt to forecast Groups 1 and 2 combined. Which is fine if these are expected to be the dominant flows across the market for the currency concerned but no use at all if the market is dominated by a firm central bank policy. Market operators tend to do this unconsciously, blithely ignoring apparently important economic data (dismissing it as irrelevant), and concentrating solely upon one group of variables.

The classic illustration of this switching of the key factors can be seen by the behaviour of sterling during the seventies. (See Graph 1 on page 136 for actual rates.)

| | |
|---|---|
| 1972–73 | Group 1 |
| 1974 | Group 3 (OPEC inflows) |
| 1975–76 | Group 1 |
| 1977–78 | Group 4* |
| 1979–80 | Group 2 'petrosterling' |

---

* At this point there occurred a major change in the emphasis of Bank of England intervention policy. The decision was taken to intervene in the market more with the objective of obtaining a steady level of sterling against the currencies of the UK trading partners in general, rather than against the dollar alone, as had been done hitherto. The measure chosen was the Bank of England's own Trade Weighted Index. The initial level of this Index was calculated based on a level of

## Flows across the Foreign Exchange Market

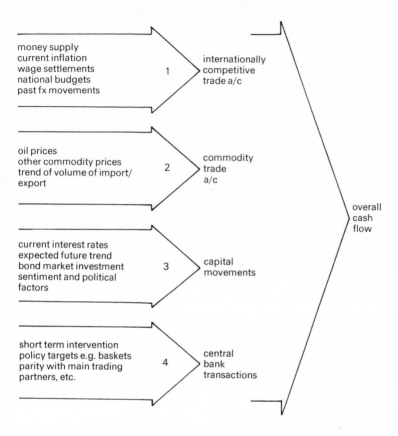

100 as at the date of the Smithsonian Agreement of December 1971 and the objective was to maintain sterling reasonably steady relative to this Index.

Throughout 1977 and 1978 this was very largely achieved in that, except for a brief period in December 1977 and January 1978, sterling was maintained constant against the Trade Weighted Index at a level of 63% with a variation over the whole period of only about plus or minus 2%.

Since throughout this same period the dollar was weakening in world markets, sterling exhibited a steady gain *vis-à-vis* the dollar, and for those who only looked at this measure of performance, sterling seemed to be doing rather well. From the point of view of the Bank of England, however, who were measuring sterling *vis-à-vis* a range of currencies, sterling was being held steady.

Other examples during the seventies were:

Deutsche Mark:   mainly Group 1, but Group 4 in the short term owing to EMS agreement constraints

Japanese Yen:   as discussed above, mainly Group 2, or 1

Saudi Riyal:   Group 4, follows SDR currency basket within close limits

To summarise:

*a*: Decide which of the four groups can be expected to dominate, ideally by talking to market dealers.

*b*: Use a forecasting method relevant to forecasting this dominant component of the market cash flow. Give less weight to other factors which impact only on other components of cash flow.

## Day-To-Day Influences

Forecasts of exchange rates are necessarily forecasts of trend lines. Actual rates fluctuate substantially from their trend line on a day-to-day basis – Graph 3 shows a typical pattern of events. Even the fluctuation within a single trading day can be quite substantial; for some currencies movements of over 3% within a trading day have occurred on a number of occasions over the last few years. What is it that causes these short term movements?

*a*: *Forecasting Economic News*

Because of the widespread awareness of the importance of news items about the economy upon exchange rates, many market dealers try to forecast economic news. Much economic data, such as balance of payments figures, retail price indices, key interest rate changes, money supply growth and so on are published to the news media on a definite schedule on dates known in advance; even at times of day known in advance. So dealers try to forecast what the numbers will look like when they are published at, say, 3 p.m. two days hence. If, for instance, US inflation figures are expected to be worse than previously, market operators will start to sell dollars to discount the news. If they are correct in their prediction, the likelihood is that the rate will move further when the news comes out as less farsighted operators see the news item on their tapes and sell as a result. This second wave of selling of course provides the first-wave sellers with a profit. But if they got their estimates wrong, the first-wave sellers will now do additional deals basing their action on the difference in the actual outturn from their estimate. That is, if the inflation figures turn out to be even worse than estimated they may do some second-wave selling as well.

All this activity in discounting prospective economic news items and reacting to actual news items is a major contributor to day-to-day fluctuations.

*b: Official Forecasts*
The publication of official forecasts of the economic prospects for particular countries can also have an impact upon exchange rates.

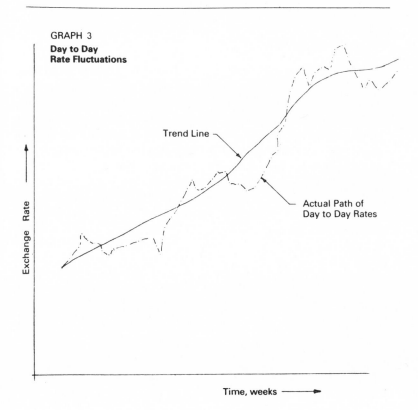

GRAPH 3
**Day to Day
Rate Fluctuations**

Trend Line

Actual Path of
Day to Day Rates

Exchange Rate

Time, weeks

Organisations such as NIESR in the UK (National Institute for Economic and Social Research), the OECD in Paris, and the EEC Commission in Brussels publish regular economic forecasts. The existence of the forecast often generates considerable comment in the financial press, all of which serves to highlight the particular economic problems and opportunities within the various economies and so influences the climate of opinion.

### c: *Political News Items*
Political news items of all types may alter the prospects for an individual currency. Such items include:
- key announcements of policy changes
- statements by senior politicians
- appointments and resignations
- public opinion polls (popularity of leaders, policy priorities, voting intention)
- elections
- trends in international relations
- trade agreements
- threatened or actual war

### d: *Technical Market Factors*
These provide a different source of day-to-day fluctuations in exchange rates.

One source arises from isolated large transactions going through the market which temporarily upset the market's ability to balance supply and demand. Like ripples spreading across a pond, the impact of the original large transaction will react around the market until the full amount can be absorbed.

Similarly, some currencies are subject to regular monthly or weekly cycles due to the impact of large regular payments, typically for oil. During 1974 and 1975 there was a pronounced monthly pattern for sterling as oil companies purchased sterling for delivery on the 15th of each month to pay for oil from the Arabian Gulf. This mid-month settlement gradually faded out as suppliers switched to dollar settlements and also introduced variable settlement dates. In 1977 there has been a regular monthly pattern in the Canadian dollar rate due to payments made by Canadian oil companies operating in the US. Gradually, market operators come to recognise these patterns and tend to discount the rate movement 'due tomorrow' ahead of time. So the pattern smooths out again for a while until some new factor arises to establish a new cyclical pattern.

### e: Position Takers

Few forecasters are also dealers. This is a pity because it is in the market that the exchange rate is decided, and market dealers come to know and recognise a number of signals and facts which are not visible to non-participants. The market has its changes of sentiment and even of fashion – it may become fashionable to suppose some particular factor to be more important than hitherto and so it will receive more attention than usual.

It may be known that a particular bank is a consistent seller of, say, Dutch guilders in large amounts, so no dealer will feel it sensible to buy guilders whilst this is in progress, however good the forecasts for Holland.

Further, the market in certain minor currencies is dominated by a few banks. Their view as to the prospects for the currency will be critical, as they can be expected to act on their view in the market, and thus cause the rate to move in line with their opinion. The small operator cannot afford to back his view against the big battalions – it is no good being logically right if the market is moving against you.

### Summary

*a*: No single economic factor provides a reliable forecast of the flow of funds across the foreign exchange markets.

*b*: In the longer term relative inflation seems to be the most significant single influence.

*c*: In the shorter term deviations from the long run trend are influenced by many interwoven factors. Most significant amongst these appear to be changes in money supply and the outlook for the current account.

*d*: Whether actual flows result in exchange rate movements is dependent upon whether the central bank chooses to offset the flows by intervention. If the central bank has a significant intervention policy, then forecasting exchange rates is principally concerned with forecasting the changing policy of the central bank.

*e*: Day to day influences are important and can move an exchange rate substantially from its trend line for short periods.

# The European Snake

## Historical

Officially 'the snake' is called 'the European System of Narrower Exchange Rate Margins'. It is a working agreement between various European states whereby they have agreed to keep their exchange rates in line with one another within close limits.

The commonly used name 'snake' is derived from the fact that when the exchange rates of member countries are plotted as a graph against a non-member currency, such as the US dollar, they move together across the page as a band of intertwined lines, resembling a snake.

The snake has its origins in the ideas of Pierre Werner, who in 1971 proposed the gradual reduction of exchange rate fluctuations between EEC currencies as one step towards eventual economic and monetary union within the EEC. These ideas had to be left in abeyance during the currency upheavals of the summer and autumn of 1971, but were taken up again following the Smithsonian Agreement of December of that year. This agreement provided a general realignment of currency values and included all of the EEC currencies. The Deutsche Mark, which had been allowed to float independently, was refixed to the US dollar. All major currencies covered by the agreement were to be held within $\pm 2\frac{1}{4}\%$ of their respective new official par values against the dollar. Thus for any pair of EEC currencies the spread between them was $\pm 4\frac{1}{2}\%$ or a maximum range of 9%.

It is not at first apparent how a spread of $2\frac{1}{4}\%$ can lead to a range of fluctuations of 9%. It is necessary to look at the example on page 130

On 'date 1' the DMark is at the top of Smithsonian band, $2\frac{1}{4}\%$ above its official central rate. The Danish krone on the same date is at the bottom of its permitted range. So the DMark is $4\frac{1}{2}\%$ higher than the Danish krone. On 'date 2' the reverse is the case;

the DMark is $4\frac{1}{2}\%$ lower than the Danish krone. So the range between any two *non-dollar* currencies has a maximum of 9%, or a band width of $\pm 4\frac{1}{2}\%$.

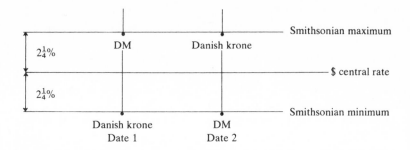

The first version of the snake stemmed from a meeting held in Basle on 10 April 1972 between the EEC Central Banks. They agreed that, in addition to the Smithsonian obligation to maintain each currency within $2\frac{1}{4}\%$ of the official dollar parity, they would in future limit fluctuations between any pair of *EEC currencies* to $\pm 2\frac{1}{4}\%$ also – half the fluctuation permitted by the Smithsonian Agreement. These arrangements came into force on 24 April 1972.

The Central Banks of the member states agreed to intervene in the market to maintain exchange rates within the margins stipulated. On a day to day basis this is achieved in the following manner. There is a system of direct telephone links between the Central Banks of the snake member states (and also EEC states not currently participating in the snake). Each morning and afternoon, according to a rota, one of the Central Banks calls all of the others on the direct line and obtains a market report, including current exchange rates and details of intervention carried out or contemplated. This process – 'concertation' in the new EEC jargon – enables the Central Banks to decide whether intervention is required and if so, how it should be handled. For instance, in which centre intervention purchases should be made and whether they should be in US dollars or in a member currency.

During the first year of operation, the EEC currencies were joined by the currencies of Sweden and Norway, whilst Italy and the UK dropped out. In more recent years France has withdrawn on two occasions. Sweden ceased to participate in August 1977.

By early 1973, there was pressure to separate the snake currencies from the dollar link and on 19 March this was done. Since that date the snake currencies have floated en bloc *vis-à-vis* the dollar but have continued to observe the requirement to keep a ±2¼% maximum spread between member currencies.

In the earlier years of the snake the Benelux members (Belgium, Netherlands and Luxembourg) further maintained their own 'snake within the snake' or, less graciously, 'the Benelux worm', by maintaining a maximum fluctuation of ±1·5% between the Belgian franc and the Netherlands guilder. (The Luxembourg franc is at par to the Belgian franc.) 'The worm' was discontinued on 15 March 1976, and thereafter these currencies behaved in the same way as other snake members.

IMPORTANT DATES IN EVOLUTION OF THE SNAKE

*1971*

| January | Telephone network set up between the central banks of EEC countries –The 'concertation network'. |
| March | Werner plan to gradually work towards economic and monetary union within the EEC. |

*1972*

| April | 24 | Basle Agreement comes into force. Participants: Belgium, Federal Republic of Germany, France, Italy, Luxembourg, Netherlands. |
| May | 1 | Accession of the United Kingdom and Denmark. |
| May | 23 | Association of Norway. |
| June | 23 | Withdrawal of the United Kingdom. |
| June | 27 | Withdrawal of Denmark. |
| Oct | 10 | Return of Denmark. |

*1973*

| Feb | 13 | Withdrawal of Italy. |
| March | 19 | Start of joint float. Interventions to maintain fixed margins against the dollar discontinued. |
| March | 19 | Association of Sweden. |
| March | 19 | Revaluation of the DMark by 3%. |
| June | 29 | Revaluation of the DMark by 5·5%. |
| Sept | 17 | Revaluation of the Netherlands guilder by 5%. |
| Nov | 16 | Revaluation of the Norwegian krone by 5%. |

*1974*

| Jan | 19 | Withdrawal of France. |

*1975*

July      10   Return of France.
Sept           Discussions opened concerning possible association
               of Switzerland. Subsequently abandoned.

*1976*

March   15   Withdrawal of France.
March   15   Benelux countries abandon their narrower margin
             system and become normal snake currencies.

*1976*

Oct      18   Revaluation of the DMark by 2%.
Oct      18   Devaluation of the Danish krone by 4%.

*1977*

April      4   Devaluation of the Swedish krona by 6%.
April      4   Devaluation of the Norwegian krone by 3%.
April      4   Devaluation of the Danish krone by 3%.
August 29   Withdrawal of Sweden.
August 29   Devaluation of the Norwegian krone by 5%.
August 29   Devaluation of the Danish krone by 5%.

*1978*

Feb      10   Devaluation of Norwegian krone by 8%.
July       6   EEC finance ministers meet in Bremen and propose
               to modify the snake mechanism to a new system
               'centred on the EUA/ECU' to be known as The
               European Monetary System or 'EMS'.
Oct      13   Revaluation of the DMark by 4%.
Oct.     13   Revaluation of the Netherlands guilder by 2%.
Oct      13   Revaluation of the Belgian franc by 2%.
Dec        8   Italy and France decide to join 'EMS', to commence
               Jan 2, 1979. Italy will have ±6% band.
Dec      12   Withdrawal of Norway.
Dec      15   Ireland decides to join EMS as from Jan 2, 1979, and
               breaks its formal link with the British pound as from
               Dec 18. UK now the only EEC country not to be a
               prospective member of EMS.

*1979*

Jan        2   Unofficial EMS intervention limit system. Members
               now Belgium and Luxembourg, Netherlands, W.
               Germany, France, Italy, Denmark and Ireland.
March   13   Official status of EMS.

*1979*

Jan      2   Unofficial EMS intervention limit system. Members
             now Belgium and Luxembourg, Netherlands, W.
             Germany, France, Italy, Denmark and Ireland.
March   13   Official status of EMS.
March   30   Ireland allows Irish pound to drift away from its
             former parity level with the British pound.
Sept    24   DMark revalues by 2%, Danish Krone devalues by
             3%.
Nov     30   Danish Krone devalues by 5%.

*1980*
No changes

*1981*
March   23   Devaluation of Italian lira by 6%.


## The European Monetary System

The old 'Snake' was officially renamed as the European Monetary
System, or 'EMS' in March 1979, and various significant modifica-
tions in its technical operation commenced from that date. It was
originally intended to become the cornerstone of a grander design
to stabilise and possibly later to unify the currencies of the EEC
countries.

The EMS is thus intended to cover a wider range of objectives
than merely the limitation of short term fluctuations between pairs
of EEC currencies. It also includes:

   *a*: A mechanism to limit movements of member currencies
       not only against each other, but also each one against the
       ECU. (The ECU, formerly called the European Com-
       mission's Unit of Account or EUA, is essentially a trade
       weighted basket of all the EEC currencies – see Appendix
       B.)

   *b*: Agreements designed to ensure that any member country
       whose currency is getting out of line with the others –
       whether stronger or weaker – is obliged to take specific
       action to correct the situation, either by intervention,
       domestic monetary or fiscal policy changes, or indeed by a
       specific realignment of its currency. Under the rules of the
       EMS, there is a 'presumption of action' when a 'threshold

of divergence' has been reached. The 'threshold' is defined as occurring when the currency's market rate against the ECU has moved by 75% of its allowable movement against another member currency. For all currencies in the EMS other than the Italian lira, the threshold comes into effect if the currency moves by more than $75\% \times 2\frac{1}{4}\% = 1\cdot 6875\%$ versus the ECU.

$c$: An elaborate network of short term and medium term swaps has been set up between the member Central Banks to provide funds for intervention under the EMS. Central Banks must intervene to maintain cross rates between member currencies within the agreed percentage limits of the central rates, normally by direct sales of the strong currency in exchange for the weak one.

These various credit lines are to commence with short term facilities of ECU 14 billion and medium term facilities of ECU 11 billion, giving an overall availability of ECU 25 billion, currently equal to approximately $35 billion.

$d$: It is intended that these swap arrangements will eventually be handled by a new European Monetary Fund, the EMF. The EMF will initially receive 20% of all gold and currency reserves of member countries, giving ECU deposits in exchange. The ECU will thus become the currency of settlement between EEC Central Banks and a new form of reserve asset.

## EMS CENTRAL RATES AND PERMITTED FLUCTUATIONS

The table on page 163 shows the 'Parity Grid' of central rates for the EMS following the Italian devaluation on 23 March 1981. It is constructed from the officially declared rates advised by the central banks for each currency against the ECU. In turn these were derived from earlier Snake parities declared against the Deutsche Mark existing in October 1978 adjusted for subsequent devaluations and revaluations. In the case of the new members, France, Italy and Ireland, the rates originally applied were derived from market rates existing as at 11 a.m. on 12 March 1979.

Two types of data are shown in the table:

$a$: The Officially Declared Rates for each currency against the ECU, shown in boxes. (See also Note 1 to the table):

e.g. France 5·99526 means 1 ECU = French francs 5·99526.

**Central Rates for EMS as Operated by Central Banks as from 23 March 1981[3]**

| | Bel./Lux. | Netherlands | Denmark | Germany |
|---|---|---|---|---|
| Belgium/Luxembourg | 40·7985[1] | | | |
| Netherlands | 14·5026 | 2·81318[1] | | |
| Denmark | 5·15186 | 0·355327 | 7·91917[1] | |
| Germany | 16·0307 | 1·10537 | 3·11165 | 2·54502[1] |
| Italy × 100[2] | 3·23048 | 0·222752 | 0·627052 | 0·201518 |
| France | 6·80512 | 0·469231 | 1·32091 | 0·424505 |
| Ireland | 59·5471 | 4·10594 | 11·5584 | 3·71457 |
| United Kingdom | Not Currently Participating | | | |

| | Italy | France | Ireland | U.K. |
|---|---|---|---|---|
| Belgium/Luxembourg | | | | |
| Netherlands | | | | |
| Denmark | | | | |
| Germany | | | | |
| Italy × 100[2] | 12·6292[1] | | | |
| France | 2·10653 | 5·99526[1] | | |
| Ireland | 18·4329 | 8·75035 | 0·685145[1] | |
| United Kingdom | Not Currently Participating | | | |

1. Central rate for currency concerned versus ECU. 'Threshold of Divergence' is reached whenever market rate versus ECU has moved more than $75\% \times 2\frac{1}{4}\% = 1·6875\%$ from this central rate. However, in the case of the Italian lira, $75\% \times 6\% = 4\%$ is tolerated.
2. Tolerance on cross rates involving the Italian lira is $\pm 6\%$ from the central rates shown. All other cross rates (except ECU see Note 1) have a permitted variation of $\pm 2\frac{1}{4}\%$ from the central rates shown.
3. Note that these rates, correct as at 23 March 1981, will alter in the event of subsequent revaluation or devaluation of member currencies.

The ECU/French franc rate must be controlled within + 1·6875% of this figure if the 'threshold' is not to be breached.

*b*: Central rates between currencies:

e.g. the cross rate between Belgium and Netherlands is shown as 14·5026. This is directly derived from the Officially Declared Rates, thus:

Central Rate = *Belgium Declared Rate*
Belgium/Netherlands Netherlands Declared Rate

$$= \frac{40 \cdot 7985}{2 \cdot 81318} = 14 \cdot 5026$$

The market cross rate must be controlled to within + 2¼% of this figure.

# Currency Baskets

The increasingly wide short term movements in foreign exchange rates have intensified the search for new ways to reduce foreign exchange risk.

As we have seen, ideally the treasurer should borrow in the currency in which he expects to receive income, and deposit the currency in which he expects to have outgoings. But this is not always possible to arrange, particularly where the currency of future cash flows is largely unknown, or is made up of many currencies.

Here the use of 'currency baskets' or 'composite currencies' seeks to achieve a stable form of international money which can spread risk and give at least an approximate means of hedging.

From the many varieties of composites that have been devised, we will select the five that have become most widely used:

the SDR
the Eurco
the ECU, 1970/2 version
the ECU, 1979 on
the Unit of Account, UA

These units command little more than a small specialised market as yet, but their importance is slowly growing.

### Special Drawing Right – SDR

The SDR has existed in four forms, with redefinitions in 1974, 1978 and 1981. The original version was created by the IMF in 1968 to provide a means of settlement of payment imbalances between central banks. It had a fixed gold value of 0·88867088 grams, then equivalent to one US dollar at the official price for gold. This 'paper gold' found a very restricted use mainly due to its patent artificiality and the rapid divergence between the 'official' and the 'market' price of gold.

So the IMF changed the valuation basis on 28 June 1974 by dropping the gold link and calculating the value of the SDR from a basket of fixed amounts of the sixteen major trading currencies within the IMF membership. The basket was revised on 1 July 1978 to include Saudi Arabia and Iran, and Denmark and South Africa were dropped.

| | 1 SDR = the sum of: | | | |
|---|---|---|---|---|
| | Definition, units of each currency | | | |
| Currencies of | 28.6.'74 to 30.6.'78 | 1.7.'78 onwards | 1.1.'81 onwards | % as at 1.1.'81 |
| United States | 0·40 | 0·40 | 0·54 | 42 |
| Germany | 0·38 | 0·32 | 0·46 | 19 |
| United Kingdom | 0·045 | 0·05 | 0·071 | 13 |
| France | 0·44 | 0·42 | 0·74 | 13 |
| Japan | 26·0 | 21·0 | 34·0 | 13 |
| Canada | 0·071 | 0·07 | – | – |
| Italy | 47·0 | 52·0 | – | – |
| Netherlands | 0·14 | 0·14 | – | – |
| Belgium | 1·60 | 1·60 | – | – |
| Sweden | 0·13 | 0·11 | – | – |
| Australia | 0·012 | 0·017 | – | – |
| Denmark | 0·11 | – | – | – |
| Norway | 0·099 | 0·10 | – | – |
| Spain | 1·1 | 1·5 | – | – |
| Austria | 0·22 | 0·28 | – | – |
| South Africa | 0·0082 | – | – | – |
| Saudi Arabia | – | 0·13 | – | – |
| Iran | – | 1·7 | – | – |
| | | | | 100 |

By 1979 it had become apparent that the sixteen currency basket was too cumbersome for ordinary commercial purposes, particularly since some of the constituent currencies had a very limited foreign exchange market. A drastic simplification down to five currencies only thus came into effect as from 1 January 1981.

As shown in the table the definition fixes the money amounts of each currency in the basket, so the percentages represented by each currency within the basket will vary from the values shown as exchange rates change.

In the period from 1968 to 1974 there had been two devaluations of the dollar (1971 and 1973) and the dollar value of 1 SDR had

risen to $1·20601. The new unit also started with a value of
$1·20601 on 28 June 1974. The dollar equivalent is calculated
each day by the IMF in Washington and is published in the
financial press. It is simply calculated from prevailing exchange
rates against the dollar, thus:

| Currency of | Weight | Market rate* $v$ $ | $ Equivalent |
|---|---|---|---|
| United States | 0·54 | 1·0000 | 0·5400 |
| Germany | 0·46 | 2·0110 | 0·2287 |
| United Kingdom | 0·071 | 2·4160 | 0·1715 |
| France | 0·74 | 4·6450 | 0·1593 |
| Japan | 34·00 | 200·60 | 0·1695 |
|  |  |  | 1 SDR = $1·2690 |

\* Market rates on 22 January 1981

The introduction of the first 'basket' basis made it possible to
calculate a market value for the SDR for the first time and the
commercial world gradually started to find uses for the new unit.
Some countries have priced their commodities in SDR rather than
in dollars; some currencies have an official par value relative to the
SDR (e.g. Saudi Arabia), and certain international agencies price
in SDRs including the Suez Canal Authority.

The advantage to the user lies in the fact that the wide spread of
currencies provides a stability of value for the SDR which is not
normally possible when investing, or trading, in a single currency.

In the summer of 1975 Chase Manhattan Bank in New York
and Hambros Bank in London started to offer a service in SDR
deposits for periods from one month to one year. Strictly, the 'SDR
deposit' is an 'SDR-indexed US dollar deposit'. The conditions of
business were initially set as:

   *a*: Minimum deposit amount US $1 million or its equivalent.

   *b*: Periods available – 1, 3, 6 and 12 months fixed deposits.

   *c*: All payments of principal and interest in US dollars.

   *d*: The principal and interest amounts due at maturity will be
   calculated by reference to the official SDR valuation
   formula current at the date when the deposit commenced.
   Currently this formula is as agreed at the IMF in June
   1974.

This will remain true even in the event that, by international agreement at the IMF, the official definition of the SDR is altered during the life of the deposit.

    *e*: Other terms and conditions as for normal Eurodollar market practice.

To illustrate the mechanics, consider a depositor placing US $1 million on six month deposit on an SDR-linked basis, and that at today's exchange rates the IMF's valuation formula gives an SDR value of

$$1 \text{ SDR} = \text{US } \$1 \cdot 2452$$

then

$$\$1\text{m} = \text{SDR } 803{,}083 \cdot 84$$

Also supposing the bank pays $6\frac{1}{4}\%$ per annum for 6 months SDRs and the period is 183 days, the interest due at maturity is:

$$\text{SDR } 803{,}083 \cdot 84 \times \frac{6 \cdot 25}{100} \times \frac{183}{360} = 25{,}514 \cdot 64$$

So maturity proceeds are

$$\text{SDR } 803{,}083 \cdot 84 + 25{,}514 \cdot 64 = 828{,}598 \cdot 48$$

Therefore, if, on maturity

$$1 \text{ SDR} = \text{US } \$1 \cdot 2475$$

The customer receives

$$828{,}598 \cdot 48 \times 1 \cdot 2475 = \$1{,}033{,}676 \cdot 60$$

This mechanism has the effect of fixing the SDR value of the funds on deposit.

    As from 1 January 1981, coincident with the simplified formulation of the SDR, a number of London banks started to offer a service in Certificates of Deposit indexed to the SDR in the same manner as outlined above.

**The Eurco**

The Eurco was originally a scaled down version of the SDR, containing only the nine currencies of the EEC member states. It works on the same principle as the SDR – that is, it consists of fixed money amounts of each currency, so that percentage make-up varies as exchange rates alter.

It provides a basket with no US dollar content, and sets out to be a European investment medium with greater inherent stability than any single European currency. One Eurco consists of:

| | | % by value<br>12 July 1978 |
|---|---|---|
| DMarks | 0·90 | 33·70 |
| French francs | 1·20 | 20·68 |
| Pounds sterling | 0·075 | 10·86 |
| Italian lire | 80·0 | 7·24 |
| Dutch guilders | 0·35 | 12·14 |
| Belgian francs | 4·50 | 10·73 |
| Danish kroner | 0·20 | 2·74 |
| Irish pounds | 0·005 | 0·72 |
| Luxembourg francs | 0·50 | 1·19 |
| | | 100 |

On 12 July 1978: One Eurco = US $1·2987

The original proportions were chosen by reference to the relative economic significance of the currencies concerned in EEC trade, as well as the relative size of the GNP of the member countries.

Like the SDR, the Eurco is a rather stable unit – even a 10% change in a currency representing 20% of the unit would only alter the value of the Eurco by 2%. Even so, it has not been widely used.

## European Currency Unit, ECU, 1970/2 version

Two versions of the ECU have been used:

| *ECU 1* | | *ECU 2* | |
|---|---|---|---|
| = FB/Lux. F. | 50 | = FB/Lux. F. | 44·8159 |
| or = FF | 5·55419 | or = FF | 5·11570 |
| or = DM | 3·66 | or = DM | 3·22250 |
| or = Guilder | 3·62 | or = Guilder | 3·24470 |
| or = Lira | 625 | or = Lira | 581·50 |
| at the investor's option | | at the investor's option | |

In both versions of the ECU the initial rates were set so that the ECU was equivalent to $1·00 in whatever the currency of measurement at the start date.

The first version of the ECU was introduced in 1970 and was intended to be a medium for indexing international bond issues. It is based on the currencies of the six original members of the European Community. The scheme provided an option to the investor to choose to be paid in any one of the six currencies at predetermined exchange rates. This meant that the value of the ECU after the issue date differed when measured in each currency at its market rate.

Several bond issues were made on an ECU basis in the years 1970–2 but it has been little used in more recent years. The fact that the investor in a ECU bond stands to make an exchange gain equal to the movement of the strongest of the six currencies and that this loss is borne by the borrower, coupled with the large exchange movements recently experienced, led to the abandonment of the ECU as a substantial borrowing medium. It simply was not possible to reconcile the interests of the investors with those of the borrowers.

**European Currency Unit, ECU, 1979 on**

Formerly the European Unit of Account, EUA, until renamed ECU during negotiation towards European Monetary System – see Appendix A. The ECU is used as a numeraire for various European Community accounting and budgetary purposes as well as being the basis of the parities for the European Monetary System. This increasing official use of the unit has caused it to become the most widely used basket after the SDR, and the likelihood that its commercial role will continue to grow.

The ECU is defined on the same principle as the SDR or Eurco, being defined as the sum of fixed amounts of each of the EEC currencies, as shown in the table on page 171.

The value of the ECU is calculated daily by the Commission and published as a rate versus Belgian francs, e.g. 1 ECU = Belgian francs 40·43 on 12 August 1980, the equivalent of $1·4170.

Because of the increasing use of the ECU by the Community, it is likely that this composite will gradually come into commercial use in the same way as the SDR has already begun to do.

| 1 ECU = the sum of | | % by value on 12 August 1980 |
| --- | --- | --- |
| DMarks | 0·828 | 32·70 |
| French francs | 1·15 | 19·65 |
| Pounds sterling | 0·0885 | 14·82 |
| Italian lire | 109·0 | 9·10 |
| Dutch guilders | 0·286 | 10·42 |
| Belgian francs | 3·66 | 9·05 |
| Danish kroner | 0·217 | 2·77 |
| Irish pounds | 0·00759 | 1·14 |
| Luxembourg francs | 0·14 | 0·35 |
| | | 100·00 |

## The Unit of Account, UA

This unit has often been a source of confusion since it is conventionally referred to as the EUA in the Eurobond and Euro-currency markets, where attempts to persuade the market to use the preferred UA abbreviation have made little headway. The UA formula was devised to avoid some of the problems encountered with the early 1971 version of the ECU, and the unit is formulated with a view to stability of value. Technically it is much more complicated than the simple baskets so far discussed. Again, there have been several versions during the evolution of the UA, but we will concern ourselves solely with the current version – 'The 9 Currency Common Market Unit of Account'.

*Value of 1 UA*
The UA is based on the nine currencies of the members of the European Economic Community. The value of the UA is defined as 0·88867088 grams of fine gold, (that is the same as the original value of 1 SDR), but this value is subject to change under certain conditions referred to on page 172.

The relation between the present value of the Unit of Account and the present Par Value (as derived from the gold values implied by the dollar parities or 'central rates' officially registered at the IMF) of each of the currencies that can qualify as Reference Currencies is:

1  UA = 48·6572  Franc (Belgium)
1  UA =  8·13822 Krone (Denmark)
1  UA =     F     Franc (France)
1  UA =  3·15665 Mark (Federal Republic of Germany)
1  UA =     F     Pound (Ireland)
1  UA =     F     Lira (Italy)
1  UA = 48·6572  Franc (Luxembourg)
1  UA =  3·35507 Guilder (Netherlands)
1  UA =     F     Pound sterling (United Kingdom)
                Values at August 1977.

'F' denotes a freely floating currency not having a par value and therefore not constituting a reference currency.

*Reference Currencies*
Reference Currencies are those currencies of the EEC countries which either have fixed parities or which are members of the European snake (See Appendix A).

*Conditions Causing a Change in Gold Value of UA*
The gold value of the UA would be changed if both of the following occurred:

  *a*: All Reference Currencies have Par Values different from their respective base values, and if

  *b*: a majority of the Reference Currencies have Par Values representing, in relation to their respective base values, a change in the same direction.

In that event the value of UA would be altered by the amount of the smallest movement experienced by the currencies in the majority.

  In practice, these conditions have never yet been met and no alteration has been made. The devaluation or revaluation of an individual currency does not alter the value of the UA, the only thing which alters is that individual currency's relationship to the UA. Other currency rates *vis-à-vis* the UA are unaltered. This is a major difference between the UA scheme and, say, the EURCO basket.

*Exchange Risk*
Whilst each of these currencies is a snake member fluctuations are limited to the $\pm 2\frac{1}{4}\%$ band of the snake. Since individual currencies

move up and down within the snake, 48·6572 Belgian francs may be more or less than 8·13822 Danish kroner on a given day and there will be an advantage in specifying the currency of payment.

In a UA denominated loan the borrower has the choice of the reference currency in which initial subscription will be made, and the investor has the choice of the reference currency in which payments of principal, premium and interest will be made.

The borrower's exchange risk is thus in practice limited to the fluctuation band of the snake. Only when all of the reference currencies change parity (and this has not yet happened), is the borrower affected by currency changes.

In all other financing structures, not only is the borrower affected by a revaluation, but more importantly by multiple re-valuations, i.e. as many as may occur during the life of his loan. It is this risk that the borrower seeks to avoid – and to which the UA goes very far to providing the solution.

The only situation where, in theory, the borrower could find himself facing a 'revaluation' risk would occur if all the reference currencies left the European $2\frac{1}{4}\%$ 'snake' and premiums greater than $2\frac{1}{4}\%$ appeared. In the event of all nine currencies floating, only the one that moved least from its official parity would be adopted as the reference for the others – the 'most stable cur-rency' clause.

The borrower has of course always the risk that his own cur-rency of revenue, with which he intends to service the loan, could be devalued, but that risk is present with any other form of foreign currency borrowing, whether done as a single currency or as a currency basket.

But, as clearly shown by the experience of the ECU, it is difficult to reconcile the conflicting interests of borrowers and investors; because of the very stability it offers borrowers, the UA is less attractive to the investor who, in today's times of changing exchange rates, increasingly seeks capital appreciation from revaluation.

# Glossary

The appended glossary is intended partly to define the many specialist words used in this book, but it also includes a great number of terms used by market dealers in their daily work. The words selected range from precise technical terms, through useful shorthands, down to plain market slang. It is not really necessary to know many of these but they are included because the reader may come across them when talking to dealers.

| | |
|---|---|
| All Current Accounting | Method of calculating Accounting Exposure which translates all balance sheet items at the current market rate. |
| Answerback | Code name of a telex subscriber, printed automatically by the telex machine at the start and finish of every message. Answerbacks are unique to the individual user and are used to identify the caller. |
| Arbitrage | 1. Dealing between two centres to make a turn in the rate due to a temporary difference in rates between the two places.<br>2. Creating funds in one currency by borrowing another and converting to that required by means of a swap deal. |
| Band | Maximum permitted range of fluctuation of a given currency against a reference currency according to an existing international agreement. |
| Bankers Payment | Payment order issued by a bank on behalf of its customer. A recipient of a bankers payment looks to the issuing bank for funds, not its customer, so the issuing bank will check that its customer has adequate funds or credit first. Bankers payments may be sent by mail or by telex transfer. |

| | |
|---|---|
| Base Currency | Every exchange rate consists of a quoted currency quoted against a base currency. The base currency is usually the dollar or sterling, e.g. in a French franc quote of 4·93 60/70 French francs per dollar the franc is the quoted currency, the base currency is the dollar. |
| Bid | Quote at which dealer buys or borrows currency. |
| Bid Market | Temporary situation where bids exceed offers at the present market rate. |
| Big Figure | The second figure after the decimal point in a price quotation. If the French franc rate against the dollar is 4·91 60/70 the big figure is one. |
| Bretton Woods | Agreement made at Bretton Woods, New Hampshire, USA, in July 1944. The agreement, signed by 44 nations, was designed to provide a stable monetary environment to facilitate the economic reconstruction of the world after World War 2. The agreement established the International Monetary Fund, and set up a fixed rate system of foreign exchange rates for nearly all the principal currencies of the world. |
| Broken Date, Odd Date | Interbank dealing is usually for fixed periods of 1, 2, 3 or 6 months with 12 months a standard period in some currencies. Any other value date (such as 4 months 6 days) is a 'broken date'. |
| Broker | Brokers match buyers and sellers, or borrowers and lenders, in the interbank market and receive a commission 'brokerage', for so doing. |
| Brokerage, 'Bro' | Commission charged to a bank by a broker. |
| Broker's Line | Direct telephone line between a broker's office and a bank's dealing room. |
| Broker's slip | Form sent from a broker to a bank, noting details of a deal transacted by the bank via the broker, and claiming brokerage. |
| Business Day | Day other than a weekend or public holiday in the city concerned. In most western countries Saturday is not a business day in foreign exchange markets. However, in Arabia Saturdays and Sundays are both business days but Friday is not. |
| Buying Rate | The rate at which the bank buys the quoted currency. |

Cable

The spot exchange rate between US dollar and sterling, e.g. 'cable is now 1·74 20/22'. This term arises from the early days of the market when a cable was sent from New York to London each day to advise the level at which the dollar was trading against sterling in New York.

Cash

Banknotes, coin, and traveller's cheques.

Certificate of Deposit (CD)

A certificate issued by a bank against currency deposited. The certificate entitles the bearer to the principal plus interest at the maturity date.

Changes

Used by dealers on telex, when a rate previously quoted changes, to indicate they are no longer prepared to deal at the old rate, e.g.

Bank A    'spot and fwds marks pls'
Bank B    '2·32 70/75
                    53–47
                    99–93
                    152–146
                    320–310
changes spot now 72–77'

Closing Rate Method

See All Current Accounting.

Concertation

Daily liaison between the central banks of the EEC countries and the non-EEC participants in the snake, to consult as to intervention policies.

Confirmation

Written advice from one counterparty in a deal to the other in which the main facts of the deal are confirmed. These would include: date on which deal done, amount plus currency dealt, whether purchase or sale, value date, agreed rate, etc. It may or may not include payment instructions.

Convertible Currency

A currency having a reasonably adequate international market through which it may be readily converted into any other currency.

Copey

Market slang for Danish krone.

Counterparty

A principal in a foreign exchange deal.

Countervalue

Where, in a foreign exchange deal, a principal buys DM500,000 against dollars at a rate of 2·40 the countervalue is $208,333·33.

Country Cheque

Any sterling cheque drawn on UK bank other than a Town cheque, which see.

| | |
|---|---|
| Cover | 1. To take out forward contracts to protect against exchange fluctuation between today's date and the due payment date.<br>2. To lay off. |
| Currency Clause | A price clause in an export contract which, for instance, specifies that the sterling sum payable for the goods shall vary in line with the market exchange rate for Swedish kronor against sterling, so as to maintain a constant value in Swedish kronor. |
| Current/Non-current Accounting | Method of calculating Accounting Exposure which translates all current assets and liabilities at present market rates of exchange but applies historical rates to fixed assets and long term liabilities. |
| Deal | A single transaction in foreign exchange. A customer calling his bank and effecting forward cover for a series of four payments due under a commercial contract, will do four 'deals', one for each date. |
| Dealing Board | The panel of communications equipment forming part of a dealer's desk. |
| Dealing Slip | Slip written out by dealer to record the deal he has done. It will show the name of the counterparty, the amount, currency, and value date, whether purchase or sale, agreed rate, and the dealer's name. It may or may not also include instructions depending on the system used by the particular bank. |
| Deposit Book | The net position arising from all deposit and loan transactions in a given currency. |
| Depot | Deposit, e.g. Depot Market = Deposit Market. |
| Depth of Market | Extent to which transactions may easily be placed in the market without causing disturbance to the rate. See 'Thin market', 'Stable market'. |
| Details | See Instructions. |
| Discount | A negative premium. See Premium. |
| DM, DMark | Deutsche Mark. |

| | |
|---|---|
| Domestic Credit Expansion (D.C.E.) | A measure of money supply designed to indicate the change in the money supply available for use within the domestic economy. In the UK, approximately equal to change in M3 minus balance of payments surplus (or plus deficit) in period. |
| Drawdown | Of loans. The drawdown is the actual payment of the loan to the borrower. This may be at a much later date than when the loan was arranged. |
| ECU | A form of currency basket – see Appendix B. |
| Either Way Price | A quote with a spread of zero. Buying rate the same as selling price. |
| EMS | European Monetary System – see Snake. |
| Escalator Clause | Clause on a medium term capital project (such as construction of a power station) to increase the money sum payable to the contractor in line with inflation. |
| EUA – European Unit of Account | A form of currency basket – see Appendix B. |
| Eurco | A form of currency basket – see Appendix B. |
| Eurocurrency | A deposit account in any major market currency where the owner of the funds is a non-resident of the country of the currency. |
| Eurodollar | A dollar deposit owned by someone other than a resident of the USA. |
| Exchange Control | Regulations restricting or forbidding certain types of foreign currency transactions by nationals. |
| Exotic Currencies, Exotics | Currencies not having a developed international market, and which are infrequently dealt. |
| Exposure, Accounting | The effect on a company resulting from a movement in a particular currency as it would show up in financial acounts. |
| Exposure, Balance Sheet | See Exposure, Translation. |
| Exposure, Economic | The economic effect on a company resulting from a movement in a particular currency. |
| Exposure, Transaction | Exposure arising from the currency cash flow of the company in the short term, say the next year. |

| | |
|---|---|
| Exposure, Translation | Exposure arising from the translation of the currency balance sheets upon consolidation of foreign subsidiaries. |
| FASB 8 | Financial Accounting Standards Board, Statement No. 8 Report by the above Board, issued in October 1975, recommending accounting treatment for foreign currency items. The recommendations are mandatory for US corporations. |
| Federal Funds | Other names: Cleared Funds, Collected Funds, Available Funds. See entry for New York Clearing House Funds. |
| Federal Reserve System | The system of twelve regional Federal Reserve Banks in the USA which carry out the role of a Central Bank. The twelve Federal Reserve Banks are: Boston, New York, Philadelphia, Cleveland, Richmond, Atlanta, Chicago, St Louis, Minneapolis, Kansas City, Dallas and San Francisco. |
| Fed. Target Range | The range of growth in monetary aggregates that is aimed at by Federal Reserve policy, e.g. 'Fed. Target Range for growth of M1' is currently 7–10% per annum. The means to this end may be another target range – e.g. 'the Fed. target rate for the interest rate on Fed. Funds is $5\frac{3}{4}\%$ to 6%.' |
| Firm Quote | Rate given at which the dealer is committed to deal, at least for a normal marketable amount. Often qualified, such as 'Firm for one million.' |
| Fixed Rate Currency | Currency having a fixed rate of exchange within narrow limits versus another reference currency, usually the dollar, sterling or the French franc. |
| Floating Rate Currency | Currency having its exchange rate determined by market forces including Central Bank intervention, but having no limits to its fluctuation relative to any reference currency. See Fixed Rate Currency. |
| FOMC | Federal Open-Market Committee. Committee that co-ordinates policy on sales of US government debt and monetary policy generally on behalf of the Federal Reserve System. FOMC meetings usually take place on the first Tuesday after the 15th of each month. |

The directives of the FOMC are made public one month after issue, e.g. the mid-January directive to the 'Manager of the System Open-Market Account' is released to the press in mid-February. Because of this, US monetary policy is open and widely debated by economists.

| | |
|---|---|
| Foreign Exchange Deal | A contract to exchange one currency for another at an agreed price for settlement on an agreed date. |
| Forex | Foreign Exchange. |
| Forward Book | The net position arising from all forward transactions in a given currency. |
| Forward Contract | Any contract for settlement later than spot date. |
| Forward – Forward Deal | 1. Simultaneous purchase and sale of one currency for different forward value dates.<br>2. Simultaneous deposit and loan of one currency for different maturity dates. This effectively provides a deposit to commence on a future date. |
| Funding Swap | See Arbitrage, 2. |
| FX | Foreign Exchange. |
| Group of Ten | A group within the IMF consisting of:<br>USA  Gt Britain<br>Germany  France<br>Italy  Japan<br>Canada  Netherlands<br>Belgium  Sweden<br>Switzerland, not an IMF member, was also associated with certain key Group of Ten meetings. |
| Hedge | Action taken by a company to reduce or eliminate a currency exposure. This includes restructuring the balance sheet, taking forward cover to match the exposure on foreign currency assets, and many other techniques. |
| Hold Account | Current account in a currency other than sterling. |
| Info Quote | Rate given for information only, without commitment by the dealer to deal at that rate. |
| Instructions | The specification of the banks at which funds shall be paid and received in settlement of a foreign exchange deal. |

| | |
|---|---|
| Interbank Deal, Market Deal | Deal where both counterparties are banks. |
| Intervention | Action taken by a Central Bank to influence the rate of exchange of its currency in the market. |
| Intra Day Limit | Limit set by bank management on the size of each dealer's Intra Day Position. |
| Intra Day Position | Open position run by a dealer within the day. Usually reduced to square or nearly so before close of business. |
| Ladder | Dealer's analysis of his forward book or deposit book showing every existing deal by maturity date, and the net position at each future date arising. |
| Lay Off | To carry out a transaction in the market to offset a previous transaction and return to a square position. |
| Libor | London Interbank Offered Rate. The rate at which principal London banks offer to lend currency (especially dollars) to one another at a given instant. Often used as a base rate for fixing interest rate on bank loans e.g. 'Interest to be fixed at $1\frac{1}{4}\%$ per annum over LIBOR'. |
| Long | Overbought position. Assets in the currency exceed liabilities. |
| M1 | Narrow definition of money supply. In the UK consists of notes and coin in circulation plus the sterling notice deposits of the private sector. See Chapter 15. |
| M2 | Measure of money supply used in the USA, defined as M1 + time deposits excluding large CDs. |
| M3 | Broad definition of money supply. In the UK consists of 'Sterling M3', which see, plus the currency deposits of UK residents. See Chapter 15. |
| Mandate | Formal authority from a customer to its banker specifying what shall constitute proper instruction for the bank to act on the customer's behalf. |
| Market Amount | The minimum amount conventionally dealt for between dealing banks either direct or via brokers. Typically \$1m or \$$\frac{1}{2}$m depending on the currency. |

| | |
|---|---|
| Marry | Where a dealer is able to match two customer deals which offset one another. |
| Matched Book | See Square Position. |
| Maturity Date | See Value Date. |
| Middle Price | Average of the buying and the selling price for a given currency. |
| Milliard | One thousand million, e.g. Yen 1,000,000,000. |
| Mio | One million. 1,000,000. |
| Mismatched Book, Mismatch Position | 1. Extent to which forward purchases differ in value date from forward sales in a given currency.<br>2. Extent to which deposits and loans differ in maturity date in a given currency. |
| MLR | Minimum Lending Rate. Minimum rate at which the Bank of England will lend to the Discount Market as lender of last resort. |
| Netting | Practice of dealing only for net amounts in a currency where a company has a two way cash flow. For example, if a company has an inflow of DM5 million and an outflow of DM2 million in a given period, then the company could 'net' and deal only for DM3 million. |
| New York Clearing House Funds | Normal basis of $ settlement of a foreign exchange or Eurodollar market contract. Provides good value for another non-US payment but is only good for a payment to a beneficiary within the USA on the following business day when the funds average from the clearing system as Federal Funds. |
| Non-Resident | An actual or legal person deemed to be resident outside the Scheduled Territories for UK Exchange Control purposes. |
| Nostro Account | A bank's account at a foreign bank, e.g. a London bank's dollar account in New York. |
| Odd Lot | Interbank dealing is usually for round amounts of, say, one million dollars. A bank wishing to deal an amount of, say, $823,604·26 to lay off a customer order would be said to be dealing an 'odd lot'. The price on an odd lot deal may not be the same as for a normal market deal. |
| Offer | Quote at which dealer sells or lends currency. |

| | |
|---|---|
| Offered Market | Temporary situation where offers exceed bids at the present market rate. |
| Open Position | Difference between total purchases and total sales in a given currency. |
| Option Contract | Forward foreign exchange contract where the customer has a right to settle on any date within a specified period. |
| Outright Deal | Exchange deal for purchase or sale of a currency for forward delivery. Term used to distinguish such a deal from a swap deal. |
| Overnight | Strictly, a deal from today until the next business day. That is, on Friday, from Friday until Monday morning. |
| Par, at Par | Premium is zero, or forward price is the same price as spot. |
| Par Value | The official parity of currency in relation to gold, or reference currency or the SDR, as notified to the International Monetary Fund. |
| Paris | Market slang for French franc. |
| Per Mille | Per thousand. One per mille is one tenth of one per cent. It may be written ‰. |
| Point | 1. One hundredth part of a cent in a price quotation, e.g. if the dollar sterling rate is 1·74 26, then a move to 1·74 28 is an increase of two points. |
| | 2. One per cent on an interest rate. That is, a change in an interest rate from 9% per annum to $9\frac{1}{2}\%$ per annum is a half point increase. |
| Premium | Difference between spot price and the price for forward settlement. Forward price = spot price − premium. |
| | A currency which is more expensive to purchase forward than spot is 'at a premium'. Negative premiums are termed discounts. |
| Proxy hedge, Proxy Deal | Dealing in, say, dollars to hedge an exposure in a currency like the Nigerian naira. This currency has virtually no market but tends to follow the dollar. So the dollar is used as a 'proxy' for the Nigerian naira. |
| Quoted Currency | See Base Currency. |

Resident

An actual or legal person deemed to be resident within the Scheduled Territories for UK Exchange Control purposes.

Risk Aversion

Measure of the extent to which a particular enterprise is prepared to tolerate uncovered exchange risk.

Rollover

1. Extension of a maturing forward contract.
2. Extension of a maturing loan, particularly in medium term Eurocurrency loans. These are often arranged 'for a period of five years with a rollover every 6 months'.

Running a Position

Keeping a long or short open position as a matter of deliberate policy in the hope of a speculative gain.

SDR

Special Drawing Right. A standard basket of sixteen currencies in fixed amounts as defined by the International Monetary Fund. See Appendix B.

Selling Rate

The rate at which the bank sells the quoted currency.

Settlement

Payment of funds on the maturity of a foreign exchange contract.

Settlement Limit

Limit on settlement risk for each counterparty.

Settlement Risk

Risk arising on a foreign exchange deal in the event of non-settlement by the counterparty.

Short

Oversold position. Liabilities in the currency exceeds assets.

Short Date

A deal for a broken date within one month after spot date.

Smithsonian Agreement

Agreement reached by the Ministers of the Group of Ten countries in the Smithsonian Institution Building, on the Mall in Washington DC on December 17/18th, 1971.

The kernel of the agreement was that there would be a dollar devaluation from $35 to $38 per ounce of gold and that many key currencies would return to fixed rates relative to the newly devalued dollar, with a permitted fluctuation margin of $2\frac{1}{4}\%$ from the new central rates.

Relative to the dollar the appreciation of major currencies was:

| Deutsche mark | +13·6% |
| Swiss franc | +13·9% |
| Dutch guilder ⎫ Belgian franc ⎭ | +11·6% |
| Sterling | +8·6% |
| French franc | +8·6% |
| Japanese yen | +16·9% |
| Swedish krona | +7·5% |

But many currencies retained their old dollar parity and the overall depreciation of the dollar worked out at around 7%.

| | |
|---|---|
| Snake | An agreement whereby certain European states have agreed to keep their exchange rates in line with one another within close limits. See Appendix A. |
| Spot | See Value Spot. |
| Spot Deal | A deal for currency for delivery two business days from today, that is 'value spot'. |
| Spot Next | A deal from the spot date until the next day, either as a deposit or a swap. |
| Spread | The difference between the selling price and the buying price. On a quote of 2·41 30/40 the spread is ten points. |
| Square Position | Purchases and sales in the currency are equal. Also called 'matched book', 'square book', and 'flat book'. |
| Stable Market | An active, high turnover market, which can absorb substantial transactions without appreciable movement in the price for the currency concerned. |
| Sterling M3 | Broad definition of money supply. In the UK, consists of M1<br>　+private sector £ time deposits<br>　+public sector £ notice deposits<br>　+public sector £ time deposits<br>　+certificates of deposit issued<br>See M1, M3. |
| Stocky | Market slang for Swedish krona. |
| Swap Deal | A simultaneous spot sale and forward purchase, or a simultaneous spot purchase and forward sale. In discussing swaps a dealer doing a simultaneous spot sale and forward purchase may say, |

'I sell and buy the currency' or may refer solely to the forward end of the deal: 'I buy in the three months', or 'I bid the threes'.

| | |
|---|---|
| Swissy | Market slang for Swiss franc. |
| Temporal Accounting | Method of calculating Accounting Exposure which translates all balance sheet items which are usually valued at cost at the exchange rate ruling at the time the cost was established, and all other items at current market rate. |
| Thin Market | A low turnover or nervous market, where an attempt to do a substantial transaction will result in a definite movement in the market rate. Spreads are wide in a thin market as dealers are apprehensive as to the rate at which they will be able to lay off any deal done. |
| Tom Next | Short for 'from tomorrow to the next day'. A deal from the next business day until the one after, either as a deposit or a swap. Note that on Friday 'tom next' is from Monday to Tuesday. |
| Town Cheque | A sterling cheque drawn on the City branch of a London clearing bank. |
| Trade Ticket | See Dealing Slip. |
| Trader, Dealer | See Deal. |
| US Quote | Exchange rate quotation on a reciprocal basis as used in the New York market until 1978, e.g. the DM is ·3979/81 dollars per DM. |
| Value Date, Value | The date agreed for settlement of an exchange transaction, e.g. 'OK, that's agreed, we buy the Guilders at 2·41 60 for value October 28', or 'The 18th is a holiday, so we are dealing for value the 19th'. |
| Value Spot | An exchange deal for settlement two working days from today. See Chapter 3 for detailed rules for determination of spot date. |
| VDU | Visual Display Unit, computer terminal. |
| Vostro Account | A foreign bank's account with a local bank, e.g. a French bank's £ account with a London bank will be a Vostro account as far as the London bank is concerned. It will also be a Nostro account as far as the French bank is concerned. |

Yard

Slang for milliard, e.g. 'I take a yard of lire' means 'I buy Lire 1,000,000,000' (at 1977 rates somewhat more than one million dollars).

# Bibliography

## Books and Official Publications

Cohninx, R. *Foreign Exchange Today,* Woodhead-Falkner, 1978

Crump, N. *ABC of the Foreign Exchanges,* Macmillan, 1963

Donaldson, J. A. *Corporate Currency Risk, The Financial Times,* 1980

Einzig, Paul *Textbook of Foreign Exchange,* Macmillan, 1966

Lesseps, M. & Morrell, J. *Foreign Exchange Rates: Theory and Practice,* Henley Centre for Forecasting, 1977

Mandich, D. R. (ed.) *Foreign Exchange Trading Techniques,* American Bankers Association, 1976

Prindl, A. R. *Foreign Exchange Risk,* John Wiley, 1976

Wainman, David *Currency Fluctuation,* Woodhead-Falkner, 1976

Weissweiller, Rudi *Foreign Exchange,* George Allen and Unwin, 1972

*Federal Accounting Standards Board Statement No. 8,* Federal Accounting Standards Board, 1975

*Accounting for Foreign Currency Transactions ED21,* Accounting Standards Committee, 1977

## Newspapers, Periodicals and Magazines

| | |
|---|---|
| *The Financial Times* | *The Economist* (weekly) |
| *'Euromoney'* (monthly) | *The Banker* (monthly) |
| | *The Bank of England Quarterly Review* |

Many international banks and certain stockbrokers in London and New York publish excellent monthly money market and foreign exchange market bulletins, but these are usually for private circulation to their own customers only.

# Index